Bootstrapping E-commerce

How to Import & Sell on Amazon

D1056564

Bootstrapping E-commerce

How to Import & Sell on Amazon

Anthony Lee
Dana Barfield

Published By: Reid & Wright Publishing
Contact: admin@reidandwrightpublishing.com
ISBN:978-0-9978553-1-9

To Andrea, Dyana and Atlantis.

And to Charlie.

Bootstrapping E-commerce: How to Import and Sell on Amazon

The contents of this book are the culmination of more than two years of research, experience and effort as well as consultations with hundreds of sellers and access to thousands of sellers' data.

CONTENTS

Bootstrapping E-commerce

How to Import & Sell on Amazon

Introduction

Anthony's Story

All my life I've had the entrepreneurial bug. I simply knew there had to be more than what I had growing up. I grew up in a lower middle-class family. I remember small houses, food rationing, and my mom tucking away money, hiding it from my dad so that she could take us on trips to the beach every few weeks. I remember being very hot or very cold and asking my mom to adjust the thermostat. She would always refuse, explaining to me that it was important to control the temperature so we could afford the utilities. I also remember wanting to snack on just a piece of bread or piece of sandwich meat and getting reprimanded for wasting food. By not making a complete sandwich I would run out of one ingredient before the other. I'm still not sure how that math adds up, but the point is we were constantly aware of how we were spending money, even the nickels and dimes. There was nothing particularly wrong with my life. It was an honorable life of hard work and occasional pleasures. But I always wanted more.

When I got old enough to start pursuing a career, I ended up dropping out of high school and very shortly thereafter, fathering my first child. While it was one of the most amazing experiences of my life, I suddenly found myself on a path that was a little too familiar. It was the path my parents ended up on; now I was there, too.

I knew that there had to be a way out. I wanted to make something more for my family. My primary goal at that time wasn't wealth; I wasn't hoping for fancy cars or a huge house. My goal was simple. I didn't want to spend my best waking hours working while missing out on what it meant to be a father to my little girl.

This led me to being introduced to network marketing and

other types of businesses that require very little starting capital. I'm pretty sure I tried them all. In fact I'm fairly certain I attempted over a dozen of these businesses.

This took the better part of a decade of my life and I failed miserably. I became so proficient at failing that I was convinced there had to be a market somewhere in the business for someone who was so good at failing. Beyond that I tried sales and found I was terrible at it. I also attempted writing and my first book flopped. Failure, failure and more failure.

So how was I making a living through all these failed business attempts? Just like my mother, I was a waiter and bartender. Needless to say, I was not living the life I wanted. I hit a few low points that were astonishing even to me. I think as we experience success in life we remember the highest points, but we also must never forget the lowest. They help us stay grounded and remind us of where we came from.

One of my lowest points was a few years ago when I lived in a trailer—yes, a trailer. Now, I was very thankful for that trailer because at least I had a roof over our heads. The problem wasn't the actual trailer but the fact that I couldn't afford to have the tank filled with gas to heat the trailer. Sound familiar? Here I was not just controlling the thermostat to keep utilities affordable. I couldn't afford them in the first place! Even in southern Alabama, it can get pretty cold in the winter months, and I vividly remember during one of the colder nights having to sleep next to my daughter to keep her warm. I can't think of a better motivator for success than that.

So I had the reason why. Now I just needed an opportunity that I could stick with until I met success. When a new form of entrepreneurship crossed my path, I was skeptical. Failure makes it hard to keep an open mind. But for some reason I decided to take a look at this last opportunity, and I'm very glad I did.

Practically overnight my mind was opened to a business type I hadn't considered—selling physical products via e-commerce through a program such as Amazon FBA. At that time, I didn't know that Amazon FBA (Fulfillment by Amazon) or any other third-party logistics programs even existed. This was a completely foreign concept to me, and, like I said, I was skeptical. But as soon as someone showed me that it was possible to have someone else fulfill your orders and handle customer returns, I realized this could be a gold mine.

I was starting from square one with this concept. I had never considered the idea of importing goods from overseas. I had no idea whatsoever how someone could manage to get their hands on any kind of inventory outside of opening their own factory. So what did I do? I studied like hell everything I could get my hands on because I had the idea that this was the lucrative business I'd been waiting for.

Fast-forward several months and I'm running an extremely successful business, consulting and helping others run businesses, and lending my expertise to services that assist e-commerce entrepreneurs as well. What? Did I say several months? Yep, I am the quintessential overnight success. However, we're going to need to talk about what success in this business actually means. More about that later. Right now I'll just say that in less than a year I managed to turn my life from the stagnant path it was on to one that was definitely pointed upward. I now set my own hours from home, and the thermostat stays at a very comfortable 73 °F. My refrigerator is stocked with food and, most importantly, my children want for nothing.

Which brings me to the two very important reasons why I'm writing this book. One, because I honestly like to help people. It feels great to cross the finish line, but for me it feels even better training people and watching *them* cross.

The second, very honest reason why I'm writing this book is because I want another income stream to support my family. Just so you know, there's a lot of bait and switch in the be-your-own-boss industry. "Experts" provide plenty of free guidance to get you excited and help you get started, but little of the nuts and bolts you need to see success. That comes with the products and courses they try to sell you after you've become a loyal follower. I'm just not a fan of that tactic. So here it is, upfront—I want your money in exchange for showing you how to build a successful business.

A word of caution about these "experts." I've followed many of them in my various business attempts and eventually I realized that most of them are people with very little experience who got lucky, saw some quick success and then decided to monetize that knowledge. What ends up happening is they give incomplete or poor advice, or spread misinformation. This leaves people not only coming up short on attaining their goals but also puts a hole in their wallets because they have to keep paying to get the next piece of the puzzle.

This isn't what you'll get from me.

How am I different? Why should you listen to me? Through some luck, lots of hard work, major obstacles, total screw-ups, and everything in between, I feel that I might be uniquely qualified to share some real, tested information on the subject of internet sales and marketing. As far as my credentials are concerned, I run a business that controls two brands, both selling on Amazon. I also consult for a handful of clients and essentially run their brands on Amazon as well.

All of this is well and good, but the most valuable information I have to offer you comes from my experience as the director of operations for ZonBlast, a product launch service that assists Amazon sellers in promoting their products and brands in order to gain visibility in the marketplace. My experience there has allowed me the opportunity to consume more data than most people in this industry. Instead of drawing only from my own products and consulting experience as most of the teachers do, I have data from thousands upon thousands of product launches. This means that I have a huge source of information that is viable and unique.

Despite that diatribe I actually don't enjoy talking about myself, so let's move into the important information in this book—the information you want most: how this can work for you. But first take a look at the optional Next Steps. Some of the softer Next Steps may or may not help you. It depends on the type of learner you are. However, I strongly suggest you complete the Next Steps pages in Part 2 and beyond, because they will help you see tangible results chapter by chapter.

Next Steps

You have a story, too. One that is driving you to read this book and inspiring you to turn the huge ship of your life in the direction you've always planned on taking. There won't be a whole lot of cheerleading here because I think too often a reader pays to learn how to do something and gets a bunch of hyped up encouragement without the substance needed to make a move. Cheerleading and inspiration may feel great for a while, but I want to give you the information you need to make things happen. That feels *really* great.

That said, it's also important to figure out why you want to embark on this endeavor to build a company from the ground up. In order to make it a success, you'll need to work hard and be committed. Not just after you read this book, but consistently, day in and day out. When you're having trouble making an order with a vendor and you're up in the middle of the night doing business because they're coming to you from Asia-Pacific time, you need to know the reason why you're doing all this.

Take a few minutes here to write down your story. Why? Because even if you *think* you know why you want to read this book and start an importing business, writing down your reason solidifies it in a way that will keep fueling your work, even on days when things aren't going as you planned. Trust me on this. When you have a bad day (and you *will* have bad days), you'll want to go back to this page to remind yourself of why you decided to take on all this extra work.

Don't overthink it. Just answer the question—why do I want to build this business?

Dana's Story

My story is a little different from Anthony's. I grew up in a middle-class family, and while I wouldn't say we were spoiled exactly, we were very comfortable. My parents did make it a point to instill strong work ethic into their three children, however. Designer jeans were never an option, not even at Christmas, and we all drove used cars and were expected to earn scholarships to college or at least chip in with part-time jobs. My struggles were always in the first-world division of struggles, the main one being to figure out what I should do with my life.

I always knew an office job wasn't for me, so as much as possible I tried to stay away from corporate life, freelancing as a writer and counseling troubled youth in an outward bound program. However, I eventually ended up in an office—a high-paced public relations firm that was mired in the bizarre world of Florida politics. After a few years of chasing down lobbyists and speechwriting, I took a break to have a child, and then went to work in the marketing division of a large health care organization. Very corporate, very intense, and ultimately, very uninspiring.

Somewhere in there, around the time I had my son, something clicked and I stopped worrying so much about where I was going and started paying attention to what was around me. Opportunities presented themselves weekly, even daily, but when headed toward a specific goal I would pass them by without consideration. When I slowed down enough to absorb the things I experienced in a day, the opportunities were obvious and I started to act on them. Looking back now, I can see that most of the really good things in my life weren't planned years in advance. They were little glimmers that flashed through the noise that I happened to grab.

My most recent glimmer was actually more like a flash of

lightning. I decided that I was finally going to take a weekend trip to New York City to explore. I hooked up with my brother, booked flights and hotel rooms, and we were on our way. We flew separately from different cities and on my first flight I scooted past a man on my way to the window seat I'd carefully selected because it was close to an exit, in a two-seat row and toward the back of the plane, which always seemed safer to me.

My point to this is, I put a lot of thought into choosing that exact seat and when I made my selection I thought, this could be a matter of life or death.

I sat down, heart pounding a bit from general travel stress, and said, "Hi, how ya doing?" That was the start of a three-hour-long conversation that was relaxed, interesting, funny, reassuring and inspirational. Both of us marveling that we were talking so much because we were not the talkative types and more apt to plug into earbuds than start up a lifelong...

A lifelong what exactly?

When we left I gave him my card, saying if you ever need a writer, look me up. A week later he gave me a call.

The feeling that something shifted in the universe bringing two people, two ideas, two lives together, is a wonderful one. It's magic. And if you believe in it, it's a feeling that can spread to everything you do, turning your work into fantastic success because you have faith. Sound a little new-agey? It isn't. It has to do with the confidence the right person or right job gives you to trust your instincts. It also has to do with a heightened awareness that allows you to see the details that are going to give you the edge when attempting a new endeavor.

In the film *Martian*, Matt Damon's astronaut character is addressing a room of astronaut trainees, and the advice he gives them is applicable to every challenge you want to undertake in your life.

At some point, everything's gonna go south on you...everything's going to go south and you're going to say, this is it. This is how I end. Now you can either accept that, or you can get to work. That's all it is. You just begin. You do the math. You solve one problem...and you solve the next one...and then the next. And if you solve enough problems, you get to come home.

Your problems might not be life or death. Your choice of a plane seat might not be life or death. But in a way they are. Not having an enjoyable, successful life that you love is a death of its own. Waking up in the morning excited to be alive...

...that's coming home.

My contribution to this book is taking Anthony's story and turning it into something that can launch the most timid potential entrepreneur into a success story that might seem out of reach but with step-by-step guidance is realistic and attainable. I've included the Next Steps sections specifically for getting the dream off the ground with real action and results. Both Anthony and I agreed that this wouldn't be a book just to pump you up with a bunch of encouragement but a step-by-step action plan to get you selling on Amazon in a way that will be sustainable for years in the future. Ultimately it's about creating the life you want for yourself. This book gives you the information as well as a little handholding as you make those first steps. What you do after that is up to you.

What This Book Isn't

It's important to define what we mean by "success." I'll tell you right now, this book isn't about how to become rich with very little effort in a short amount of time.

As a matter of fact I'm going to go a step further and assure you that this book does not promise financial freedom within a few months, and maybe not even within a few years.

Many business books will tell you such success is possible, even likely, with hard work. They go on to tell you that if you just put in 12 months of effort, you'll see promising results. Many readers take that to mean they should see at least some results after just a few months. I lucked out, others luck out, but that's not always the case.

Here's the thing: I'm over a year in the business that I'm in and I have yet to spend a single dime on myself or my family. Don't forget, I'm my own boss because I figured out a way to take what I learned building the business and help others do the same. "What am I reading this for then?" you're probably asking. Don't close the book yet. I'll explain.

I haven't taken any money out of my business because I choose to reinvest everything I make so I can build a legacy for my family.

This book isn't going to be the nuts and bolts of how to go out there and make fast cash. This book is the nuts and bolts of how to build something that you own, that you control and that can provide you with stability in the future. How far in the future that is, I don't know, and very possibly you won't know for a while either.

Of course, there are always the special cases. The ones who have the golden touch and just somehow jump into the business and become wildly successful in an extremely short period of time. There are a few who manage this, and maybe you'll be one of them, but the vast majority of people will stumble a few times, especially if they try to go too fast.

Rather than gamble and plunge in head first, I suggest making solid plans with realistic goals to build something for a brighter tomorrow. I would like to provide you with the construction material to do so. You may not make millions with the information I teach you, but it is completely possible, even probable, that years down the road you'll find yourself standing on the solid foundation of a life you can be proud of. Hopefully, you look back and remember this book as the one that showed you the way.

If you're looking for a lot of ra-ra and big promises, this is probably not the book for you. If you want the step-by-step nuts and bolts, without further ado, here we go.

Next Steps

After that reality check, let's do something truly inspiring. Brainstorm names for your new business. How to set up a business entity will be discussed later on, but coming up with names is just fun!

What to Expect

I'd like to go over a little bit about what you can expect from this book. You can expect detailed information on the exact steps that someone else has successfully taken to build a physical product e-commerce business. You can expect very specific guidance, such as how to find the right product to sell; how to find and negotiate with a supplier overseas; how to navigate through logistics; how to build a brand around that product; and much more.

You can expect to learn exactly what I learned over the course of the last couple of years building my own business, dealing with some serious hurdles, seeing quick unbelievable sales and then experiencing a major drop in sales. You'll learn about what I learned when I started helping others build their businesses. I'll tell you one thing. When I first started consulting, I failed miserably. That failure led to a formula that now helps me and my clients successfully launch physical products on Amazon, again and again. I will give you that formula.

What you can expect from me is a lot of honesty. I'm not asking you to trust me, but I am asking that you give me the opportunity to earn your trust. I'll do that by sharing the highs and lows, the good and bad. Basically, this is an unfiltered account of how a former bartender managed to build a multiple six-figure business from the ground up on a shoestring budget.

One thing I will say is that I most certainly did not do this on my own. In that decade of failed business attempts, I was operating from a lone wolf perspective. It was when I finally accepted the idea that I should let others help me that things started taking off.

A lot of the ideas that I will present in this book are the result of a collective effort. I give a great deal of credit to a small mastermind group that has helped me learn everything I know about this business. Now you can expect to learn the same.

The method I teach in this book of selling on Amazon utilizes their FBA program (Fulfillment by Amazon). This program allows you to send your goods to Amazon and *they* take over the responsibility of sending the products out when customers order them, handling returns, and all the other hassles of fulfillment.

That said, I will *not* be going over the tiny details of how to set up an account, what settings to set, how to create a shipment, how to submit tickets in seller central, etc. There are many books that go over that information, and besides, every bit of it is freely available on Amazon's own website or YouTube.

So you will see me reference things that you will only truly understand once you sign up for a professional selling account on Amazon, create your first listing and send inventory into FBA.

Next Steps

Anthony told you what you can expect from him. Now write down what you can expect from yourself. Jot down the number of hours you can realistically commit to the business. Are you able to travel? Do you have startup funds available? (If you don't have funds, don't worry. That will be addressed later on in the book.) Nothing about your situation is prohibitive. Any obstacle can be overcome, but it's important to have a clear perception of your starting point.

One More Thing

There is one more thing that I want to mention. Just about everybody that I've ever met who has wanted to start a business from home approaches the business with the same goal—to make some extra money so they can eventually replace their current income. They always say, "If I could just make $5000 a month, I'll be okay." I did the same thing. I had the idea that if I could sell $10,000 or $15,000 worth of product on Amazon and keep half of it, I'd have it made, working from home and living the dream. I have to be the bearer of bad news here. Every person I've ever known who has taken money out of their business to fund their life has regretted it. I went into the game with the same goal in mind, but I realized quickly that the rules of this game are very different from what I first imagined.

If a business gets to the point where it's actually growing, you have to put more in to expand. That means that all that money you'd like to pay yourself needs to go into more inventory, new and different products, marketing your brand, or other opportunities that will secure the future of the business.

I think this is the single largest illusion about this business that gets shattered. As I said earlier, I have yet to take a single dime out of my businesses. In fact, now more than ever, I am interested in expanding, and I'll tell you why.

Expansion is the business education with the most value. When you learn what it takes to build a real business, that's when you'll be ready to create a legacy for your family. You will learn this very quickly the first or second time you run out of inventory.

So I just wanted to dispel any of those hopeful notions that a lot of the other gurus capitalize on. I don't want you to think this book is going to be your key to replacing your job in the next six months, even if you currently make $3000 a month. Understand that you may very well decide to stay at your job for a year or two while you grow your business.

At some point, hopefully sooner rather than later, you will realize that to build a successful business you have to constantly reinvest, and every dime you remove weakens your ability to grow faster. This isn't a bad thing. When the time comes you'll be happy to make that decision because you'll know you're working toward your future. Your normal day (or night) job will stop feeling like a grind. As you sit in your office or work truck or whatever it is that you do, you'll smile when you look at your Amazon sales and realize that in a single day you just made $500, $800 or even $1000. And even though you're not taking any of that money for yourself, you could. And take it from me: just knowing that it's there makes a world of difference as you go about your day. It's going to feel good knowing that you're capable of achieving that kind of income and that when you're ready to cut yourself a salary, you'll truly be your own boss.

Next Steps

Write down where you want to be two years from now. Five years? Ten? It might be hard to think that far ahead, and no doubt things will change between now and then, but to have a general direction to go in is important. What are those big things you want to accomplish? The safety net of an extra income? A new home? Your child's college education? Retirement? Write them down now and refer to this page often. Make adjustments as your goals change over the years.

Part One:

The Business of Importing

Why Import

Perhaps the most important aspect of building a physical products e-commerce business is the concept of buying low and selling higher by leveraging the worldwide marketplace. Basically, you'll learn how to do what I did—import products at extraordinarily reasonable prices, add modifications to make them unique and sell them at added value on Amazon.

A lot of people may have mixed emotions when it comes to importing. They feel that these goods should be purchased domestically in order to contribute to their local economy. I can tell you now that this is not a lucrative mindset for a business owner. As a business owner, all economies are worth supporting, and you go where you can get the highest quality for the best price. Other countries also have differing infrastructure or real estate allocated to certain specializations, making them more qualified to provide you with certain products.

China, for example, has a *lot* of land allocated for industry. They have a tremendous number of factories, and their government subsidizes the production of goods for export. This is why China manufactures 80 percent of the world's air conditioners and 70 percent of the world's cell phones.

Meanwhile, here in America, we have much less land designated for factories because we use most of our real estate to grow food. Importing not only makes sense, but can be a great contributor to the global economy.

How It Works

This book is about how to become an importer and sell products on Amazon. Actually, to be perfectly accurate, you will create a company that will be the importer. Your company will be listed as the importer of record and consignee when the importing transaction occurs.

Importing involves researching a product and seller (most likely overseas), purchasing that product, coordinating branding at the factory and shipment to a fulfillment center in the U.S. (in this case Amazon). By the time your product arrives at the fulfillment center, you'll have set up a listing on Amazon including photos, keywords and product description and be ready with an awesome launch strategy. There are numerous tiny steps to take from the time you start researching a product to the first payment that lands in your bank account, and they will be covered in this book. For now, this chapter will give you an overview of what the business entails. Don't forget, we are here to walk you through every step of the way, so if any of the information on the next few pages sounds daunting, know that all will be explained. By the end of this book you will be fluent in the language of importing.

Because you are starting an import business it is very important that you familiarize yourself with things such as tariff codes, duties and taxes, FDA requirements should you decide to import anything that needs FDA approval, and any other regulatory certifications necessary. I won't go into them all now, but when you're ready to decide on a product, flip to the list in the Appendix and familiarize yourself with the basic requirements. Depending on your situation you may find certifications not listed in this book so be sure you do enough research on your own to be sure your business is handling your product in the proper way. The easiest way to do this is to search for importing case studies for your particular product. These will clue you in to the more specific nuances and give you a heads-up as to what you can expect.

Incidentally, these regulations aren't confined to the world of importing. You will not only be an importer but also a retailer. As a retailer you need to know the laws that regulate what you are allowed to sell. For example, should you decide to sell baby products, you should know that in the United States you are required to have your baby products pass certain safety tests. These requirements will vary by product, niche, category, etc. But it is extremely important that you familiarize yourself with what is required.

Next Steps

Did any of what you just read make you nervous and feel as if importing might not be for you? List those things here. As you continue reading, refer back to this list and as each of these issues is addressed, check it off. Before you know it, you'll realize you're becoming an expert and that importing is no more intimidating than any other new skill that comes with a learning curve.

Private Labeling

To really dive into how this business works we have to touch on something extremely fundamental. First of all, we've been talking a lot about importing your own products, and I want to emphasize what "your own" actually means in this book. We're not talking about importing KitchenAid products to sell, or any other brand name product. What we mean by your product and your own brand is what is referred to as private label, or white label, products. If you're coming to the importing business brand new like I was, you might think it entails inventing and manufacturing your own product. While you can do that if you want to and have the resources, an easier way is private labeling.

To understand private labeling, first you have to understand factories. Once upon a time I used to believe that a factory was a company that grew big enough to warrant a larger manufacturing facility, but at that time I didn't understand much about business. Business is actually all about filling needs. The best way for a business to function is to do what it knows how to do best.

If you find what you can do best, and use that to fill a need, that is the way to amazing prosperity and the same is true for factories. The most efficient way for many factories to operate is to mass produce certain products and allow others to come in and make them their own with specific tailoring and branding. This way, they are always producing and they have a much larger pool of goods to offer the marketplace for sale.

A manufacturer can make aesthetic and physical changes to the products that they currently manufacture for the purpose of creating a unique branded product for a company. Major corporations do this all the time. When you go to your local grocery store you may notice that the store has its own brand of certain food products. They do not actually produce their own ketchup, mustard, paper towels and milk. They simply put their label on the product.

Manufacturers refer to this as either OEM (original equipment manufacturer) or ODM (original design manufacturer) manufacturing. But the common term for this is private labeling. The factory serves as the designer and manufacturer of a specific product, giving you the opportunity to improve upon the original design, or simply add your branding to it.

For example, a private label manufacturer might make beautiful bamboo cutting boards. You may decide that your company will specialize in kitchen products and want to offer a bamboo cutting board. You then talk to the manufacturer and find out they can do a couple of things you want. They can cut the shape of the board to be something entirely unique. Perhaps the shape will enhance the function and make your product more desirable than others on the market. Another option is to have the manufacturer burn your brand onto the board. This doesn't change the functionality of the board, but it does change its aesthetics. In some instances you may not find it feasible to add your branding to the product itself. In that case, you can simply have the product delivered in branded packaging.

These are the capabilities of OEM and ODM manufacturing. They give you, the small business person, an opportunity to leverage the experience and quality of an established factory, and gives them the opportunity to produce goods for sale.

How Much Money Do I Need to Start?

Now to the bottom line and what we all want to know. How much money do you need to get started? The truth is you can ask any number of gurus and experts and they will all give you a different response. Most of the ones peddling courses will try to tell you that can do it all for $300 or less. They do that so they can get more people to sign up for the course. Others say it can be done for less than $5000. I tend to agree a little bit more with that figure, but even so, it will vary wildly, so don't let that number turn you off. The truth is, the amount of money you come up with up front will depend on your strategy. For example, you may want to start by selling a small handful of unbranded samples. This will allow you to verify the product's market viability, and generate a little extra seed money. If you choose to go that route, and you luck out and choose a great product from the start, you could actually start your venture with very little capital.

So yes, there are those who have managed to build their importing business on just a few hundred dollars. Understand, however, that this will take a lot longer. For those of you who can start with a larger bankroll, you can achieve more results at a faster pace.

Let's look at the other end of the spectrum. If you walk into this with $50,000 to invest, you'll be able to purchase all the inventory necessary to float your business for six months before reorder and marketing expenses kick in.

If you have $50,000 floating around, great. But I sure didn't. Most people will probably fall somewhere in between these extremes and there are always work-arounds. Here's how I managed it. I opened three credit cards. I used one credit card to purchase the course that taught me about how to sell things on Amazon, another credit card purchased my initial inventory, and the third credit card paid for business setup, marketing, website, trademark and other ancillary expenses. All in all, my startup costs were around $11,000. If you take the course out of the equation it was about $7,500. Also keep in mind, I chose a very expensive product to import. Many people choose a product that costs just a few dollars per unit. My products cost me a significantly more than that.

So the answer to the question "How much will this cost?" is that there is no concrete answer. It depends on the price of the product, your patience and your strategy. The good news is if you have next to no money, there is hope. If you have a pretty significant bankroll, you'll get there fast. And if you're like me, and find yourself somewhere in between, things should go just fine.

I will say this, however. If you know that you have a viable product that has been tested and tried in its respective market, you want to start with as much capital as possible. The reason for this is because the less money you start with, the longer you'll be playing catch-up trying to get enough inventory to keep up with demand. This is why most of my colleagues initially shot well past me with their success. While they were all able to replenish their stores quickly, I was depending on sales to stock inventory for a year. Had I been able to start with about $30,000, I would have seen the numbers that I'm seeing now within my first 90 days. So keep that in mind.

I don't suggest that you get a significant loan, or take out a bunch of credit cards like I did, unless you are 100 percent confident in the market for your product. This is why it's wise to consider testing the market with samples first. If you don't have experience in a specific market, or marketing in general, then taking extra steps to verify your product and demographic choices may be best. But if you have a small amount of business acumen, a background in marketing and understand how to conduct market research, and your product choice is based on that and not on emotion, I say go all in. That is precisely what I did, and I never looked back.

Next Steps

List your resources.

Cash:

Credit cards:

Investors:

How much are you willing to invest in your startup?

Business Setup

If you want to start a business of any kind, it's important to set it up correctly from day one. I want to briefly touch on the topic of business entities and starting your business legally. This is in no way intended to be legal, accounting or tax advice. These are simply suggestions based on my own personal experience. The first suggestion is to obtain an employer identification number (EIN). This is your tax ID. It's extraordinarily important to have one of these so that the proper entity is taxed at the correct rate.

Furthermore you actually have to have an EIN in order to import goods. Luckily the United States government gives away EIN numbers for free. Once you obtain an EIN the next logical step is to actually start your business entity. Most people go with the simple limited liability company (LLC), but you should consult with a tax professional first before you make that decision. A professional will be able to assess your future goals and determine what will work best for you in the long run.

I want to give you an advanced tip at this point, one that would've been extremely helpful for me to understand in the beginning. When you realize that your tax ID number gives your company its own individual identity, then you might decide to set up multiple corporations that will allow you to structure things in the best possible way to ensure the most efficient payment of taxes.

What I mean by that is if you plan on growing in multiple directions, or even if you don't plan, but it ends up happening, then you may realize you'll need one company and many subsidiaries. That's where I find myself right now. I always thought I would only have one company, but now it looks like the best route for me is to allow a holdings company to distribute services through a variety of other entities.

Aside from selling physical goods on Amazon, my company also engages in consulting and publishing. So keep that in mind when developing your long-term strategy and make sure that the accounting and tax preparation consultants that you choose are competent enough to understand how to set these types of things up.

After you have a business entity created, that business entity will need a bank account. These are minor details that I strongly suggest taking care of as quickly as possible. When you have an entity with a tax ID and its own bank account, then you will be able to move forward with all necessary business proceedings. Another advanced tip is to make sure that the bank that you choose to do your business banking offers an easy to use and affordable solution for making regular overseas wire transfers. Thankfully, I accidentally chose my bank well. But I have a client who didn't. His first major shipment actually had to be made with PayPal because he could not get his bank to facilitate the wire transfer. That was a very expensive and unfortunate mistake.

When you go to sit down with the business banker make sure that you asked what solutions they can offer you that allow you to make regular wire transfers overseas. After that's set up, you are quite literally in business.

Setting up your business entity is actually not complicated and you can do it yourself. However, there are legal organizations, or rather organizations that have agreements with law firms that can assist you. They cost a little bit more than doing it yourself, but they will ensure you get the paperwork filed correctly the first time, and sometimes they'll even provide you with the education you need to make informed decisions as you set up your business.

A note of housekeeping—I will also recommend that you make the decision to purchase accounting software at this time. The best thing for you to do is have a meeting with the person you hired to handle your accounting and ask their firm what software they work best with. Many will say QuickBooks but whatever software they are used to using, that's the one you want. That way the people in the accounting office will be able to easily log in and help you with things on your accounting software remotely. Once this is set up, and as long as you're keeping track of all of your expenses and general business record keeping, you'll only have to do a quarterly review to make sure everything is accounting as it should.

The most important thing is that you have a business that is able to import goods and quickly and easily wire funds for those goods to other banks internationally.

Next Steps

Apply for an EIN. This is easily accomplished online at irs.gov for free. A simple search for "obtain EIN" will guide you.

Find a CPA in your area and schedule an appointment to discuss a new business setup. Before your appointment familiarize yourself with the different business entities LLC, C Corp and S Corp. Which one do you think will be best for your company?

Part Two:

Getting Started

Finding a Product

Finding a product to sell is probably one of the most exciting and challenging parts of running this business. Maybe you're teeming with ideas and have all kinds of inspiration, or maybe you have no clue where to begin. Either way, it's all new territory, ripe for exploration. Choosing a product is the first step toward the destiny of your choosing.Many people believe that the product you choose to sell is the most important thing and that your product will determine your success or failure. I don't agree with that sentiment at all. I look around online and I see people selling *everything*. The craziest thing on the internet is being sold, and likely in enough volume (by at least one seller) to make a decent profit. That doesn't mean it's impossible to pick a product that fails. What it means is, there is a careful balance you need to consider. A very popular product already has demand, but a *lot* of competition; whereas a less popular product has little competition, but lacks a great deal of volume.

I believe you can sell whatever you want and make it a success —eventually. However, you would probably prefer the fastest route to success, so let's choose a product with that end in mind.

The Future of Your Brand

Another thing to consider is the future. Selling a great product is fantastic, but what happens when you've gone as far as you can with it? What do you do next? An important part of my process is choosing products that fit into a brand that has growth potential. What I mean is, when I choose a product, I choose one that generates ideas for complementary products as well. That way I can quickly expand into new products within that brand as soon as the sales start coming in.

Also, an important distinction that you need to make early on is that you are *not* selling a product, but a market. Sure, you can sell a widget. Anybody can really. But growth and stability come when you serve a need that a sizeable population shares. By serving a market, you can more easily understand the needs of your target customer and find the most effective way to get your brand in front of them. This will also aid you in discovering what new problems you can solve for your customers.

The Novel and Unique—and a Little about Patents

One effective way to find something awesome to sell is to find something novel and unique. Every approach to finding a great product to sell has its own obstacles. The major obstacle for this one is patents. Finding something novel and unique, and otherwise not found for sale in very many places, can often mean this invention has been patented. In case you didn't know, you can't sell a patented item as your own product. That's a very quick way to go out of business. However, you can find something unique that is either not patented, or has been changed enough from its patent. Then you might be able to enter the marketplace with an extremely profitable product.

If mass production factories overseas make significant improvements and changes to a patented product, then you can resell it without infringing on the patents. Needless to say, this technique must be approached with caution. When you find an interesting looking product, the first thing you must do is look for the company that sells the product and find out if they hold the patents. Look carefully for mention of patents in the product description. You may find patents for very similar items. For example, you'll find a patent for a three-in-one can opener. However, you may also be looking at a four-in-one can opener that is an improvement on the original design with the new functionality making it a completely unique product. This is the winner you want: a unique product inspired by a patented product but not patented itself, allowing you to sell it for big profits.

Another thing you can look for is whether or not the manufacturer holds a patent on the item. This is because an overseas patent will not hold any legal power in the United States, but if they have a patent that typically means they are the designer. So if your research leads you to a product that doesn't seem to have a patent, but the manufacturer who offers the product holds a patent for it, you may have found a winner.

Now when I say unique and novel, what I mean is something handy. To give you some examples, a rolling pin with nubs that perforate the dough, or leave cool shape indentions. When that product first came out, it was likely very popular and profitable. The life straw is another good example. It is an extremely saturated market now, but when it first came out, it was likely very profitable for early adopters.

These items were either too general to have their own patent, or easy enough to modify for their own unique version.

The Hot and Popular

By far the riskiest of product selection methods is going after the hot, new, and extremely popular. Why is this risky? Because of all the competition. If you decide to go into cell phone cases, not only will you be competing with hundreds of other third-party sellers, but you'll also be competing with dozens of very large and established brands.

Another downside is that these products are often obsolete after a few months. What is hot now never remains so, as something newer and hotter is always on the way.

Despite these negative points, one reason people flock to these types of products is because they are proven. You don't have to concern yourself with whether or not people will want to buy your product, because they are already buying them in truckloads from other sellers.

The key to entering this kind of market is capital. You need money, and lots of it. The reason is because you'll have to advertise more, promote more, and have more inventory than your competitors to take a piece of their market share. This is a costly game, but if you have the funds to see it through, you can build a very profitable business.

The Unsexy

There is one method of choosing a product that many don't consider, but is extremely lucrative; it just takes more time. This method is to steer away from what people want and move into what they need—unsexy things that you probably won't make a fortune on, but when you have a large catalog of these unsexy necessary products, you start to build a very stable and profitable company. These products are easy to find. Just take a look in your house and take note of all the things that you use. Look on your sink in the kitchen; what do you see? The soap dispenser with an attached sponge holder. Very unsexy, but I guarantee you people are buying these off of Amazon.

In my house we also have a cork board. As a business owner I don't think I would ever decide to sell cork boards, but if you think about it, plenty of homes have them. We also have a pretty generic glass candelabra in the middle of our kitchen table. These are all examples of items you may not initially think you want to build a brand around, but focusing on things people need as opposed what they want is a good way to build a very stable and evergreen company. You will be far less susceptible to competition moving in and taking a piece of your market share. You'll also be far less susceptible to seasonal fluctuations. A single product like that may not generate any more than $5000 a month in sales, but if you have 100 of them you will be doing very well.

First to Market

The concept behind this method is that you are trying to be the first person to the market with a product. This method is basically combining the novel and unique method with the hot and popular method. Essentially, you are looking for novel and unique products that are the newest improvements on already hot products.

Usually you won't come across these as a newbie seller. These are typically brought to your attention in your supplier's new catalog or at a trade show or fair. These are the *next* new awesome thing.

For example, as of this writing virtual reality (VR) headsets illustrate perfectly what I am talking about. People were just getting excited about big systems like the Oculus Rift and then the cell accessory manufacturers came up with a terrific idea—create an inexpensive headset that simply holds your mobile phone to your face, allowing people to take advantage of the VR technology they already own.

To illustrate further, imagine the Lifeproof case when it came out. Before it there were only cases that protected phones from being dropped. And everyone has a case, right? So then waterproof cases came out, they were a huge hit.

In both instances, what was the key? Getting to the market with these products before everyone else. Why? As mobile devices evolve and new versions come out, these items in their original form will become obsolete. So the key is to get them up for sale as soon as possible before they are no longer desirable.

The big risk here is that you are testing an unproven market. These products may be improvements or modifications of things that are already popular, but not every modification is adopted widely.

The big obstacle for this method is getting your product as quickly as possible. This means you'll need short production times and few modifications. While these are important factors, you still can't sacrifice quality or brand image. So again, there is a careful balance.

Little Competition

Regardless of what method you choose, the key is to find a product with as little competition as possible while still having decent demand. The reason for this is that most products on the Amazon marketplace have a lifespan when the product makes decent sales. As more and more competition moves into a market, that lifespan decreases. There is a point of utter saturation when even the oldest and most established brands lose a tremendous amount of their sales. You extend that lifespan if you move into a market as far away from that point of saturation as possible.

Ground Rules to Get You Started

1. It's a good idea to start with just one product. While it is true that having many products in your catalog will lead to higher profits in the future, getting your feet wet with one product will help you lose less money during your learning curve. First, you may find the expenses are greater than you anticipated. Next, if you make any glaring mistakes or run into any serious challenges, they are easier to fix or recover from with one product. So, get that first product going first and then move onto multiple others once you have the hang of things.

2. Consider your passion. I know it is cliché to talk about how if you do something you love it doesn't feel like work, and that's not what I'm saying here. The reason I suggest going after products you have great interest in is because it will make your target demographic, or your avatar, easier to market to. For instance, if you're a new parent, you're probably super passionate about the role. You've put a ton of thought into all the gadgets and other essentials you want to buy for your baby. You've also likely identified some of the shortcomings of products in the market and are familiar with the challenges that brings. Knowing your avatar intimately (because you fit the demographic yourself), you'll be able to choose a product targeted to a waiting buyer.

3. Do as much research as you can on your "avatar." An avatar, as mentioned above, is the picture of your ideal customer. This is the person most likely to say a resounding *yes* every time they are presented with the opportunity to buy what you offer. Ideally you'll be a close match to this avatar, but you are still only one person. You need to understand your avatar in every possible way. Get to know how your avatar acts in a statistical setting. Learn their buying habits, their preferences, their tastes, their average income, their gender, the amount of time they spend online, how much they buy

off Amazon. The more you know, the greater your arsenal for launching your brand and getting your customers' attention.

4. Start with the end in mind. When you pick your first product, be sure to pick one that will fit in a catalog of branded products you'll eventually offer. Yes, it is possible to make six, and even seven figures selling one product online. However, growing a brand and diversifying helps to build stability for your business and ultimately your income.

5. Don't get too attached. I know, I just told you to start with your passion. You do want to have a deeper understanding of your products. However, you cannot choose one and decide *this is the ultimate, number one, most important product we'll ever sell and I'll stick with it until I make it work*. I mean, you can, but sometimes a product just isn't in high enough demand, and you may lack the skills necessary to create the demand. For the good of your business you have to be able to move on if necessary.

Identifying Your Awesome Product

Regardless, to start you're simply coming up with a list of ideas. Ideally you've got a niche or product type (or maybe a couple) in mind, and those will give you a good place to begin your search. One of the best places to kick this off is with the search functions in Google, Amazon and eBay. If you type in a single word relating to your niche, auto-complete will fill in results based on popular searches. You can get a tremendous number of ideas from that alone. For example, here is what Amazon's suggestive search gives when you type in the word "baby" (see figure 2-1).

Figure 2-1: Amazon's suggestive search for "baby."

You may find an item or two and then decide to cross-reference them with Google Trends (google.com/trends). This is a separate search function within Google that shows what terms have been trending recently. It will show you the search volume of a term over time, the demographics of those conducting the search and related terms. This is a good way to identify a product that has been growing in interest. For example, if you look up garcinia cambogia, the supplement Dr. Oz plugged as a weight-loss miracle, you'll find it had almost no search traffic from 2005 to 2012 (see Figure 2-2). Then suddenly there's a huge spike between 2013 and 2014. The point is Google Trends is a great tool for identifying a product of major interest.

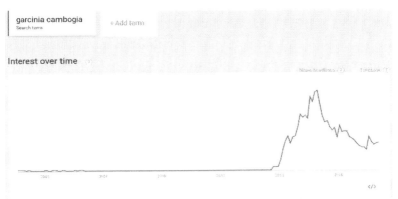

Figure 2-2: Amazon search traffic for garcinia cambogia.

Amazon also has a wealth of information that is useful. For example, Amazon bestseller lists will show you the top products in any category. The top 100 is a great place to find really hot products. However, these are often very competitive markets. If you look at a top 100 list and see nothing but products with more than 1000 reviews, that presents a challenge. Changing your search to products ranked in the top 500 to 2000 reduces your competition to medium to low level. If the products in that range have fewer than 400 reviews, then you stand a good chance of competing in Amazon sales for that project.

You can also look at the top items in subcategories. Sometimes it can be profitable to drill down into smaller niche items. While this reduces the number of daily sales, as some items just don't get that much volume, you may still be able to obliterate the competition and get to the top of those subcategories.

Another great way to use Amazon as a filter is to look at the "most-wished-for" items in a given category. This is a great way to find in-demand, novel items straight from buyers themselves.

eBay also offers a great resource for product information, but not on the site itself. eBay is such a large marketplace, with so many eager sellers and auctioneers, that there are entire websites dedicated to helping potential eBay sellers find the top selling products.

Sites like BestSellingAuctions give you a list of all the categories and then rank each item's popularity based on bids and watches. Then there is WatchCount, where you can type in a keyword and the site serves up a list of items and their past sales.

You will find that there are plenty of great products to research and consider, and these tools should give you plenty of resources to find the best product to start your business. Remember to start with one, but have a few in mind for future growth. When you've narrowed down your search to a few strong candidates, it will be time to look for suppliers.

Anthony's Personal Criteria for Finding Products

These are my personal rules that I stick to when I'm looking for a product to import. Don't let this set of criteria confuse you. These are not set-in-stone ground rules. I know many people who have been successful with a product that breaks at least one of these rules. I am simply showing you my thought process. If you find a product that fits one of these categories and it is a good product and one you feel confident you can market, then by all means make an exception.

Nothing "oversized" by Amazon's standards. The reason is because oversized products take up more space and can be heavier. This will cause shipping prices to be much more expensive. Furthermore, if you sell via Amazon FBA, they limit your inventory storage to 500 units and charge ridiculous storage fees. While this creates a great barrier of entry against your prospective competition, it may offer too many obstacles for someone just starting out.

No electronics. Many of my colleagues are making a killing with electronic items. I just prefer to minimize the number of returns or defective products I will encounter, so I recommend establishing yourself before going this route.

Nothing breakable. Use your best judgment about what's breakable. I try not to choose products that are prone to damage during shipping.

No consumables (supplements, skin care, etc.). We are talking about importing here. Many other countries don't have the same standards as we do for consumables and the FDA adds a new layer of challenges in customs.

Nothing that comes in varying sizes or colors. Now, this is a tough one. I actually have a product that comes in varying colors, but starting out, simple is better. In the beginning you'll probably only be able to afford one color or size, so you may lose out to your competition if they have more of a selection.

Try to stay away from anything with moving parts. For the same reason I stay away from electronics and breakable things, I simply want to minimize returns of damaged and defective goods.

I want to reiterate, these are suggestions based on my preferences, but I can name at least one person selling over

$20,000 a month with at least one product that fits each of these categories, including "oversized" products, so take these criteria as guidelines only.

A Note about Restricted Categories on Amazon

Some categories on Amazon are "restricted," meaning they regulate who gets to sell in them. These categories vary and so do their barriers of entry. They are not insurmountable. Amazon is very up-front about what categories are restricted and what they expect of you to get approval. While this book won't go into detail about every restricted category, there are some general requirements that are easy enough to meet. For example, a few categories require three receipts (invoices) from different vendors. You simply find the item you want to sell elsewhere and buy it. Don't mention anything about private labeling, just purchase the item from a retailer and submit it. Some requirements ask for photos. These will be easy enough to provide so long as you have the item in your physical possession (which you should if you got samples). You may need an official website and shopping cart for your product. This, too, is pretty easy. You can build your own WordPress site, hire someone to do that for you, or sign up for a service such as Squarespace that offers a drag and drop template to build a simple site. Also, Shopify or a WordPress plugin can provide you with a shopping cart.

In the end, if you find your product is in a restricted category, don't be deterred. The hoops you'll have to jump through are actually a good thing because it slows competition down. Only serious players are likely to go through the hassle of getting approval, so the pool won't be as crowded.

Next Steps

Choose a demographic you know well. Define it by gender, age, income range, location, and anything else you can think of that will distinguish these buyers from the rest of the market. Drill down until you have fully fleshed out your perfect avatar. **(Example: mothers: females, ages 18-45, income of $35,000-$75,000)**

List items to sell to this demographic that you're interested in or passionate about. The higher the level of passion the better. Do you love to cook? How about a kitchen tool? Do you love parenting? How about that baby item you've been looking for everywhere but can't find?

By using the tools in this chapter, choose a product you're passionate about with a target demographic you understand, with minimal to moderate competition and moderate to high interest in search results. This could be an excellent choice for your first product!

Researching the Competition

Now it's time to talk about one of the most important steps in this whole process—competitor research. Researching your potential competition is crucial to gaining a better understanding of your market. You want to research your potential competition before you decide fully on a product, and once you decide on a product, you'll want to do even more research. Knowing your competition inside and out gives you ideas on how to best market your products and helps you to understand the marketplace better as it pertains to your niche. Amazon provides a number of tools that will help you in this process. They won't give you everything about your competition, but they will provide you with some valuable data that you will use going forward with your business plan.

First type your product keywords in the Amazon search field and pay attention to everything that shows up on page one. These are the people you want to compete with the most because the goal is to make it to page one for your most profitable keywords.

Take a look at the number of reviews for each of the different products. Pay close attention to how established the competitors are. This will give you an idea of how much effort it will take to pass them in sales. Ask these key questions:

Are these mostly large brands or are they third-party sellers?

Do they have thousands of reviews or only a few?

Questions like these help paint the picture of the amount of effort, time and money it will take to compete. For example, large brands with brand recognition may seem difficult to compete with, but it all depends on whether or not anyone at the company puts effort into their Amazon presence. This is easy to determine by simply looking at their listing.

Sellers with thousands of reviews will be difficult to displace from their top positions. While I believe that with the right branding and marketing just about any product in any category can be a success, I would recommend not attempting to enter a market where everyone on page one is an established seller with thousands of reviews.

The next thing you want to look at is the Amazon bestseller rank (BSR). The BSR is a trailing indicator, but an important one as it tells you how much sales volume the product gets. BSR numbers vary in the message that they send from category to category. However, you can quickly determine if the product you've chosen has a lot of interest by looking at these numbers. On the Amazon platform, the lower the BSR the more popular the product and the more sales it makes. Just as it would be very difficult to compete with an entire page full of products under 100 BSR, it also might not be a good idea to go into a product where everything on the first page for your primary keyword is over 10,000 BSR. A good mid-range for bestseller rank is between 500 and 2000. However, up to around 8000 can provide respectable sales depending on the price of your product.

Next, you'll want to read the reviews. This will give you an idea of the things customers like and don't like about this type of product. Reading the positive reviews will give you an idea of what is absolutely necessary for your product to possess. You definitely don't want your product to lack any key features that everyone else in the market is promoting. Reading the negative reviews will give you an idea of the types of pitfalls you may run into. It also will give you valuable information about improvements that will make your product superior. Definitely spend considerable time reading through all of your competitors' reviews.

You'll also want to scrutinize your competitors' listings. There are several reasons for this. First, it allows you to see many of the major keywords that your competitors are using in their listing copy. You'll see how they're being creative, or how they're lacking creativity in their imagery, and you'll get a good idea of the level of attention the sellers are paying to their listings. You'll notice, for example, that a lot of bigger companies have extremely thin, bare-bones listings. These listings have very little copy, no description, and only one image. That is because the majority of their sales come from outside of Amazon, and therefore the platform isn't a priority for them. This is the easiest competitor to overtake in rankings. If you see a lot of well-written listings, then you have a much better idea of the amount of effort you'll have to put into keeping your listing fresh.

You'll also want to move off of Amazon and look at your competitors' websites. Do this to get a better idea of how established your competition is. This research will also paint a good picture of how established you'll need to appear and give you a good idea of other types of products you may consider in the future.

Next, take a look on YouTube for videos related to your competitors' products. This will give you the ability to look at marketing material that may exist for your competitor. It will also give you a better sense of what customers think about the products.

Paying close attention to the customer gives you a heightened sense of the market. Once you have a really good idea of who will be buying your product, you need to learn as much about them as possible. Google the demographics' buying habits. Look up their social media profiles. See what types of pictures, status updates and restaurants they frequent—everything you can possibly find out. The more you know about your potential customer the more powerful you can make your message as a brand. This will permeate not only your brand image, but all of your marketing materials as well.

Next Steps

Search for your product on Amazon and take a good look at what shows up on the first page.

Are they mostly big brands or third-party sellers?

Ask the following questions of each product:
How many reviews does it have?

Good reviews?

Bad reviews?

What is the listing like? Long and descriptive? Short and lacking in important details, or somewhere in between?

What is the best seller rank (BSR)? To find this number, scroll down a product listing to **Product Details**.

When you read the reviews, what are three things that customers will expect?

What are three things that customers want but aren't getting?

A good way to quickly tap into a demographic's social media profile is to follow groups. For example, if you're interested in mothers ages 18 to 45 with an income of $35,000 to $75,000, follow one of the many mommy blogs out there that matches this demographic. Research your demographic and write a 100-word description of your potential buyer. Do they work? One job or three? Do they have an active social life? What are the things that are most important to them? Include the details that stood out to you as you perused their social media profiles. What does your buyer want most?

Branding

Let's now dive into exactly what it means to brand a product. As we discussed before, many factories make products that have no branding or are otherwise generic with respect to branding and offer entrepreneurs the ability to modify the design of the existing product to fit their own company identity. This is much more efficient than trying to design your own products from scratch. The amount of money, time, research, prototyping and data that goes into developing a new product is pretty extreme. Now, it is a good idea to be creating something you can call your own, but until you have grown to a point where you can afford this endeavor, better to start with already established concepts.

Brand markings can be directly applied to a product right there during manufacturing. Your logo or brand name can be stitched, etched, heat stamped or otherwise affixed to the body of your new private label product. This is ideal for a few reasons, chief among them, so it is harder for people to imitate and create counterfeit offers. In some instances, however, it may not be possible to apply your brand markings directly to your product. That is ok. In these instances, you can simply have custom packaging designed.

Right now is a good time to starting thinking about your unique branding strategy. In our daily lives we are inundated with branding, yet many of us probably don't have a clue how exactly to create a brand from scratch. The brand is the identity of your company. Imagine a brand is a person you would recognize on sight or by the sound of her voice, or some other distinguishing characteristic that you associate with that person. Brands work in much the same way. Brand logos often become symbols that we recognize immediately. Before even seeing the name of the brand, the logo conjures the brand's qualities in our minds. You can take any major brand and see what I mean. If you see the Nike swoosh, for example, you know that the brand represents athleticism, and your mind might conjure up images of a sweating athlete or any number of products that the brand sells.

When you create your brand, you will be creating a memorable and recognizable symbol in the name and logo. The first step is naming the brand. This name doesn't necessarily have to be your company name. For example, if your company is XYZ Wellness LLC, the brand name might be Superior Health Supplements. The important thing about the branding is that it is consistent with the image you want your company and its products to portray and conveys the message that you would like your prospective buyers to receive. It's not so important that the brand name be catchy so much as it needs to have depth conveying what its products have to offer.

Once your brand has a name, then it will need a logo. The logo can simply be the brand name in a special font, or it can have a symbol associated with it. Ideally you've already been playing around with different symbols and artwork, but if you're stuck you do have resources at your disposal. For example, there are companies like 99designs that are full of talented designers ready to create a logo for you. 99designs even allows you to run a contest giving prospective designers the opportunity to compete with their design ideas for your business.

If you already have an idea of what you'd like your logo to look like but you're not a designer, sources such as PeoplePerHour, fiverr, Upwork and a number of others give you access to skilled freelancers and contractors that will help make your vision a reality.

Another thing to consider when creating your brand is what colors you want to use. Branding doesn't stop at the name and logo. The colors are also very important because they create a mood. Font, too, is important. These elements will come into play when you put together a website for your company or brand. This may sound like a lot to consider but it really isn't. All you have to do is look at your favorite brands. Look at competing brands. Look at their websites and study their colors, fonts and design qualities. Is it a simple, spare look? Or is it full of flourishes and artistic elements? As you study other brands you'll begin to formulate your own vision. Then, when you work closely with a designer, you'll be able to put together something that you'll fall in love with.

When you are ready to sell on Amazon, your company name will be the name that you use as your seller name. Your brand, or brands, will be registered for the products they represent. The logo, banners and any other graphics will be uploaded in your marketing, ads and seller profile. That uniformity will add to your credibility and make your company look much more professional. It may take a little time to put together an awesome brand but definitely don't skip this step and put some thought into it so you can maximize the impact it will have on potential buyers. Looking professional with an aesthetic and intriguing representation will increase buyers not only on Amazon but anywhere your brand interacts with people.

One element of branding that most people are concerned about is trademark. You're probably wondering if it's necessary to register one. The answer is, not right away. Understand that trademarks are only for specific product categories, specific word phrases, and specific markings. So it can be a little difficult to determine at the beginning exactly what trademarks you will need. I would recommend, however, that you take care of this as soon as you are able to. Not because it's a requirement for your business to be successful, but because it will help you in certain situations that you're going to find yourself in while selling on Amazon. Registering a trademark protects your intellectual property, and when dealing with online marketplaces it's best to have all the protection you can get. So my advice is this: after your company experiences a little bit of success, you can move forward with registering your trademark for the various aspects of your branding. Trademarks will also increase your credibility and put you in a much stronger position to protect future marketing efforts as your company grows.

Next Steps

Choose three of your favorite brands and visit their websites. Note the general feel, colors, fonts and anything else that stands out to you. Pay attention to the general impression you get from each one. Does one of these brands accomplish the effect you would like your brand to accomplish?

Go back to your brainstorm of business names. Choose the one or two you like the most. Jot down your thoughts about the following branding elements for each.

Name:

Logo design:

Colors:

Fonts:

Name:

Logo design:

Colors:

Fonts:

More about Private Labeling

Private labeling is a viable business option that anyone can take advantage of. You don't have to be a large company to private label and the process is simple. When you place your order for products overseas you have your manufacturer either include your brand identity on the product itself, or on custom packaging, so your logo, company name, color scheme, and other branding elements are included on your product somewhere during the manufacturing process. If you sell a textile product, for example, this could mean your logo is stitched right on the product. If you sell a plastic product, your logo and brand name might be printed on the product. If your product is glass, you may have custom packaging made with your brand identity on it. It could be a custom box, or simply a custom cardboard tag stapled to the top of a plastic bag.

A note on packaging: I recommend that if there is a way for you to put your brand name or logo directly on the product, you should. The more distinct you can make your product, the better it is for your brand, especially when regarding protection of your trademark. However, in some instance this may not be an option and then you have to think seriously about packaging. I have seen many businesses with fairly standard products charge premium price and get away with it. How? Because they had amazing packaging. Most people in this industry preach selling at premium prices, and I'm not disagreeing with that, but you will need to offer a feature that commands that price. This can often be the type of packaging. Outstanding packaging can account for an increase in your profit margin from 10 percent to as much as 50 percent. When I say outstanding packaging, I don't mean a standard box that has great graphics; everybody does that. But if you're willing to spend three or four dollars for a box that is as nice as what an iPhone comes in, then you can probably double your price.

Premium packaging may not be feasible in the beginning, however, and that's okay. When I started, my products came in a plain polybag. As your brand grows, however, you'll want to start heading in that direction.

The next hurdle will be deciding where to get this packaging. The first thing most people do is try to find a packaging factory. There are many in the U.S., but they are usually pretty expensive. Also, labor for doing the packing is pretty expensive over here. You can source packaging overseas in the same way you do your products. However, that may not be necessary. If you do a good job finding a factory and supplier, they will likely have the ability to offer custom packaging, and usually it's inexpensive. Two of my own suppliers offered a free box. Whether or not it was free or the price was rolled into the entire price, I don't know, but both of those products are packaged in custom boxes with beautiful graphics. I wanted to get a really fancy corrugated box for another of my products. My factory didn't make them, and I thought I would have to source from a box manufacturer, but my factory had an arrangement with a box maker already for their other packaging. They gave them my design specs and had them manufacture the boxes and deliver them back to the factory where they boxed the product right there. The total cost per box with the labor of packing each item was 35 cents.

This is just one more thing to keep in mind when you're selecting a supplier. If custom packaging is going to be important to your brand, make sure you make it one of your requirements.

You have plenty of options, but understand that the point in the process where your brand identity is added is at the manufacturing level. This is something you'll need to keep in mind when placing an order. You'll need to make sure that the manufacturer offers OEM or ODM products. You want to be able to sell your own branded products, and you may even want to be able to make changes to the product in the future. There may be features that you discover are missing from other products that you could add to your own to make it more appealing to buyers. Private labeling gives you this control.

Next Steps

Is there something you use every day that you think is great but would be even greater if it had this one feature? There are likely others who feel the same way and *you* could be the one to offer the world this improved product. List up to ten products you would like to customize. Get creative and have fun with this exercise. Use this new list of products to enhance the products you came up with earlier.

Part Three:

Acquiring Your Product

Finding Your Supplier

This next phase is one of the most crucial parts of the whole process. The right supplier can literally make your business. By the same token, the wrong supplier can take the wind right out of your sails. For a bootstrapping newbie entrepreneur like I was, that would have been game over. As mentioned before, there is always risk involved with any business venture. However, those risks can be substantially greater when you are dealing with people that you physically cannot meet in person. That means your communication skills will have to be spot-on.

There are many different ways to vet a supplier. Some methods are more effective and provide more security than others. However, there is no foolproof way. You can take extra measures and be extremely careful and still get burned. On the flipside, you can stumble onto a great supplier and get totally lucky. In the end, you simply have to do what makes you comfortable with putting money on the line.

In the beginning there are several common questions that come up regarding finding overseas suppliers:

Where do I look?

Is there a master list of trusted suppliers out there?

Are there any countries I should stay away from?

The first two questions are intertwined, since "where to look" also means which websites compile master lists of suppliers. While there are many websites out there that offer access to overseas suppliers, I can only speak with confidence about a couple. I have experience with Alibaba and know of many sellers who have successfully used TTNET. Most of what follows is the procedure I used to vet suppliers through Alibaba, but the same strategies should work for TTNET as well. I will also mention a few other, similar sites, but I cannot speak to their effectiveness or safety. A quick search online will find forums and reviews where others will speak to their good and bad qualities.

As far as what countries to stay away from, I have to warn you. Most overseas factories with a generic item manufacturing business are in China. There are other countries in the mix, but only for very specific items. For example, if you want weight lifting straps, you'll be buying those from Afghanistan. Lots of fashion accessories like scarves come from India, and you'll find plenty of bedding in Turkey. The point is it doesn't matter where the product comes from. The important thing is the supplier and your relationship with them.

Choosing a B2B Site

So let's get down to it. Where do you look for suppliers? There are a few websites with the sole purpose of connecting business buyers with business sellers. While most of these sites offer a level of security in their vetting process, your job is to sift through the pile of options to get to the seller that suits you the best. This will require due diligence, and a certain level of perpetual paranoia. The most popular of business-to-business (B2B) sites that feature overseas suppliers is Alibaba. They have been a giant in this space for years. A lesser known site is TTNET. They mimic Alibaba in a lot of ways, but they are not as big and their services aren't as feature-rich. I have never personally connected with a supplier from TTNET but Perry Belcher, author of the book *Import Export Business: How to Import from China Using (O.P.M.) Other People's Money*, claims to have experience with the site. Other popular sites are HKTDC, and Made-in-China.

These sites all essentially operate in the same way. They act as a bridge between manufacturers and would-be buyers. They offer premium listing placement for a price that yields a **Gold Supplier**, **Royal Supplier** or **Gold Member** badge. These badges are supposed to indicate a level of trust between the website and the manufacturer, but really it only shows that they purchased an upgraded membership. Even so, this badge, along with other inspections, site checks and indicators, can be used to help ferret out a good supplier.

My personal favorite B2B site is Global Sources. Global Sources has been around much longer than Alibaba, and they have a more airtight vetting process for their suppliers. When a supplier on their site is stamped as "verified" this is not the same as on Alibaba where most suppliers pay money for the certification. Verified suppliers on Global Sources have their business license, and all entities and locations have been physically checked. Paperwork is double and triple verified and a representative visits the business site to have a conversation in person with the representative of the business.

Aside from the "verified" tag, other pertinent information is published, such as trade shows. You can review the shows your prospective supplier attends regularly and where to find them next. Many businesses also undergo a credit check. That way you can see that the supplier is in good financial health.

The Global Sources website functions are also very user friendly, allowing you to refine your search through a number of filters. My favorite filter is "manufacturer." This means you can filter out all of the traders, distributers, agents and middlemen, leaving you with the information you need the most.

The site also provides a "Buyer Support" tab that offers a number of experts who will answer your questions about importing.

Next Steps

Visit alibaba.com, ttnet.net, hktdc.com, made-in-china.com and globalsources.com. Make notes about your impressions of each. Which are easiest to navigate?

Which one has a large selection of the products you're interested in?

Which one makes you excited to jump in and start buying?

Choose a B2B site and get ready to find your supplier.

What to Look for in a Supplier

The first thing I look for is whether the supplier is a **Gold Supplier** (Alibaba), **Royal Supplier** (TTNET), **Gold Member** (Made-In-China), or **Verified** (Global Sources). These are indicators that a supplier has a higher level of trust. It really is just a way for these sites to charge money. They charge suppliers thousands of dollars a year to be premium members, putting a gold badge on their profile and including them in lists of trusted suppliers. So, why is this the number one indicator you should be looking at if it's a bought credential? Because you'll only want to deal with a supplier that has been a premium member for at least three years. If it's a fly-by-night scam operation, likely they won't foot the bill for even one year of membership. If they did pay, they would certainly either be long gone or found out by year two. Three-year premium members have been able to continue to pay thousands of dollars a year and stay in the good graces of the website. This helps you narrow the pool down to the most likely honest candidates.

Next, look at reviews or complaints. All sites like these have the ability to review the supplier. Let me be clear that very few suppliers have reviews, but if they have any, be sure to look at them. Alibaba also recently added an indicator that shows whether a supplier has had any complaints in the last 90 days.

Then Google the name of the company and look to see if anyone has filled out a Ripoff Report or reported them to any other scam-exposing sites. You'll be able to use your judgment as to whether you want to work with someone based on how many negative reviews you find about them on the internet.

You'll also want to look for the supplier's website. Many of these B2B or "bridge" sites (because they create a bridge between the supplier and buyer) offer a subdomain to suppliers, or they may have their own business site. Either way, look at their website and gather as much information as possible. Look for pictures of their facility and an address and phone number. Basically, look for all the things a legitimate business with nothing to hide would have. Another thing you can do if your prospective supplier has an external website is to Google the domain's whois information. Simply type **whois:** and their URL in Google, and you will be served with info about who owns the domain name, how long it has been registered, where the site's servers are located and even email addresses associated with the website. If things here look on the up and up, you're doing well in your initial vetting process.

Google the names of the supplier's representatives to see if you can find social media profiles. This may seem like stalking, but supplier sites often provide the first and last name of the rep you can contact. Use that name (or any others you can find) as your search focus to find social media profiles. It won't always happen, but if you find them on LinkedIn, for example, with a short description about how they are a rep for the company, that's a good sign.

Look to see if they attend trade shows. China, specifically, is home to some of the biggest trade shows in the world. Most suppliers, especially the ones that do a lot of international business, will display their booth information on their website or B2B page. Scammers don't typically pay to be a part of a trade show, so this lends credibility.

Look to see if they accept secured payment options. On Alibaba, for example, there is a resource called **Escrow Services** where money is paid into an Alibaba account and the supplier does not receive it until they confirm shipment of your product with tracking information. This service, and others like it, is somewhat costly and it may not be feasible to use, but if your supplier accepts it as a payment source, that is a good sign.

Next Steps

Now that you've found a B2B site you feel comfortable using, start looking for suppliers. Make a list of five that sound pretty good and answer the following questions for each one:

Are they a credentialed supplier on that B2B site (i.e., **Gold Supplier** on Alibaba)?

Have they had any complaints or bad reviews?

Do they have good reviews?

Are you able to find professional looking social media pages for the supplier rep?

Do they have a website?

Does the website look like one a reputable company would have?

Have they attended trade shows?

Negotiating the Deal

Once you've identified a handful of suppliers that look promising, the next step is to start communicating with them. It's time to take the plunge and reach out by email as a representative of your company. You can do this in a couple of different ways. You can represent yourself as the business owner, which is perfectly fine, or you can represent yourself as an executive for the company, which is fine too. The most important thing is to not come across as an amateur.

Understand that suppliers field a lot of tire kickers and a lot of people who will waste their time. At the end of the day they are employees in a sales position. That means they have to quickly sift through all of the inquiries, get to the cream of the crop and negotiate a deal. The best way for you to get their attention is to represent yourself professionally as a legitimate buyer, because that's exactly what you are.

That also means you need to do your research. A lot of people don't realize that the people on the other side of these websites can actually see how much time you spent on the website researching the products that they offer. They also pay attention to how much you know about the actual product, *and* they will do the research on *you*. If all you do is a broad search for some type of product, write up a very generic inquiry and cut, paste and send it to 50 people, all of them will know that you did that, and they probably won't take you seriously. I have included a template in the Appendix that is my introductory email to suppliers. But aside from using the right words in your email you need to actually show some interest.

Do your research and get to know the products that they offer. Then when you write your email, represent yourself as somebody who is there to do business and knows exactly what it is they're looking for. When you write your introductory email you want to avoid the urge to jump straight into asking about price. Most of the time price is highly negotiable, but you will only get the best prices after you have established a relationship with your supplier. An effective way to do that is to ask them if they have samples available before you ask about price. Ask them if they have the ability to send you a representation of their work right away. That sends the message that your primary concern is quality.

Next Steps

Use the template to draft a personalized inquiry to the suppliers you're interested in, send and wait for their response. You're on your way to negotiating your first deal!

Samples

At the end of the day the absolute best way to secure a good supplier and a quality product is to focus on getting the highest quality products at the best possible price. In order to do that you need to get the goods in hand. Using the inquiry template I provide, ask for samples and find out how quickly the supplier can get them to you. If you did your research, you've already sifted through the candidates and picked the most promising ones, so it shouldn't be a waste of time and money to go ahead and pay for samples. Ask three or four suppliers for samples of a product that you are sure you want to sell. Then take the highest quality. If you're lucky, at least two will be of high quality. Then you can choose the best price.

I remember when I did this for the first time, I was talking to three suppliers on a regular basis. One of them really stood out, and I was totally convinced I would do business with them. I loved everything they had to say and everything they had to offer. However, I knew it would be wise to get samples from at least three suppliers so that I could really be sure that I was comparing quality. Even before I got the samples I was certain that I would do business with this one supplier. Another supplier's sample arrived and their quality was not up to par at all. It was an easy decision to drop them. Now it was between the one that I knew I wanted to do business with and the other one that had a cheaper product that I was sure wouldn't be good enough. As it turned out, the one I wanted to do business with was actually manufacturing a product that had a patent on it in the U.S. They were manufacturing counterfeits! I'm very glad that I discovered this because I would have been in hot water had I moved forward with that supplier. Luckily, the supplier that had the cheaper product that I thought would be totally subpar was actually the highest quality out of the bunch.

So always leave yourself with a handful of options and don't make a final decision until you see the product yourself. Take delivery of your samples, compare them and weed out the ones that don't meet your standards. The ones that impress you move to the next round. Then you start to negotiate on price.

A Note on Sample Price and Delivery

Chances are, the factory you're dealing with has an established account with a major courier (likely DHL). That means they get much better shipping rates than you can. For this reason, when you ask for a sample quote, you'll want to ask for the shipping to be included.

Many times, the shipping price you pay will be negligible, but sometimes you don't get quoted the best shipping price. This throws a lot of people off. They might be confused why the sample is going to cost them $150. They may think they are getting ripped off. To dispel that, I can confirm that sometimes it will cost that much. This is just the price of doing business.

Another thing that throws people off is that sometimes you'll get offered a sample for free and sometimes they'll cost $50. Again, you aren't getting ripped off. Many times these higher sample prices are put in place to weed out tire kickers. Typically you can ask to have the price of the sample deducted from the price of your bulk order should you choose to do business with that factory.

Next Steps

Decide on a budget for samples and order what you can from the suppliers that are showing the most potential.

Pay for your sample using PayPal or Western Union.

When your samples arrive, inspect them with an objective eye. Don't be surprised if what you get isn't what you expected.

Negotiations

When entering into negotiations, make sure that you ask for prices of much higher quantities than you actually intend to buy. If they think you're going to place a 5,000 or 10,000 unit order then they are more likely to believe that you're a large company and know what you're doing. I've provided a template in the Appendix that shows what my follow-up email looks like. Remember, you now have a relationship with this supplier because you've already ordered a product. Now, you're simply asking your supplier to provide you with standard pricing on large quantities. Along with that you need to really hammer down the details. Make sure that the price they give you includes any customization that you'll be requiring, including packaging, logo and any modifications that you identified during the sample process. The more customization you make, the longer the sample process will be, but that's OK because the more hoops that your supplier jumps through, the more committed they'll be to negotiating a deal you're happy with.

When you get the prices make sure you also pay attention to how responsive your supplier is. It doesn't matter if their factory offers the highest quality and the best price if you can never get the rep to contact you. If you find the perfect product and the rep is terrible, submit a new inquiry through the original website and try to get a different rep. It is extremely important that whomever you're dealing with is very available to you, because, in a way, they are going to become your business partner.

As a side note, I only like to deal with the manufacturer directly. I do not like dealing with trade companies or distributors because they have much less leeway when it comes to the pricing. Ideally you will be dealing with a manufacturer who is capable of making any modifications or customizations that you need while giving you a fair price.

At this point you'll probably be ready to make a decision as to where to place your first order. Don't burn any bridges with your other potential suppliers, because you never know when you'll want to switch. Simply send them a polite letter stating that, while you thoroughly enjoyed the quality of their product, at this time you were able to secure better pricing. If the pricing is not terribly far off, this is also a really good way to get the supplier you *want* to do business with to lower their price. You can pit deals against each other by going to a supplier and saying something like this:

I spoke with my colleagues, and we have decided on a budget. While I prefer your quality, and I would rather do business with you, we got an offer from another supplier that was a much better price. If there's any way that you can extend to us a price that is at least as good, we will most certainly place our first order with you.

That haggling trick works just about every time. As a matter of fact even if I don't have another offer that's better I will usually tell the supplier I like that I do. I can typically knock off at least 20 to 30 cents per unit that way. Once you've negotiated the deal you have solidified a relationship with the supplier. They've sent you a good sample, they've been highly communicative with you and they've met your ideal price. From this point everything should go smoothly for your first bulk order.

Next Steps

Request prices for at least 5,000 units. As you're getting prices, take note of how communications are going.

Does your rep get back to you quickly? Are there many misunderstandings?

Once you find a supplier with a price you like, let them know that you have a better price you're considering, and watch them knock a little more off per unit.

Dealing with Manufacturers, Traders and Agents

As I mentioned, I prefer to deal directly with a manufacturer as I feel this gives me the best chance at a fantastic price, as well as making modifications or custom products in the future. That said, sometimes you don't find the factory directly. Sometimes the factory that makes the product you are looking for doesn't advertise, and you'll only manage to reach a trading agent.

Dealing with a trading agent isn't necessarily terrible. On one hand, you are going to end up paying a middleman. But on the other, they might be able to negotiate better prices than you could. Also, they may be able to communicate your customizations better since they speak the language. So don't rule out a trading agent entirely.

Along the same vein, you may decide to work with a sourcing agent. This is an agent who works directly for you, rather than the factory. Their job is to find you a factory, negotiate the best price, communicate custom modifications and see the deal all the way to the end. They typically take a percentage of your order, but you may find their assistance worth it because often they can accomplish a lot more than you can. This is because they are there, visiting the factory, shaking hands with the factory managers. Face time does matter in this business.

Just know that you have a lot of options, and it's all a matter of how many points along your supply chain make sense. The fewer parts, the less it costs, but adding agents into the mix can sometimes offer you more flexibility. You just have to see what will work best for your company.

Placing the Order

The final stage in this process is placing that order. Likely you told your supplier to quote you a price for a much larger order than you want. Now that you're working with an established relationship, you can say that the first order has to be a test order to make sure that the transaction goes smoothly and that the market accepts the quality of the product. This will usually work all the way down to an order as small as 500 units. I don't recommend trying to go smaller.

When you place your order, the standard for most overseas transactions is to deposit 30 percent, so they can obtain the raw materials to manufacture your order. The remaining 70 percent will be deposited once they show you proof that they're ready to ship. The easiest and most accepted way to handle these deposits is via wire transfer. Some of the bigger importers use contracts such as letters of credit that help protect their assets a little more. Typically these contracts cost more money and are used for much larger orders. Smaller companies usually do what's called a telegraphic transfer (TT), which is a wire transfer. The escrow service some of the bridge websites offer is an option but are also usually expensive. For example Alibaba's escrow service costs 5 percent. Alternatively, sometimes you can use PayPal, but their transaction cost is 4 percent. In my experience, the most affordable way is simply to do a wire transfer through your bank. Transfers usually don't cost more than $25 or $30.

As a side note, your method of payment for samples will probably not be a wire transfer, because paying a $25 fee on a sample is a little unnecessary (especially when the sample itself likely cost that much). PayPal and Western Union are my favorite ways to pay for samples, although keep in mind that Western Union isn't as secure when dealing with small quantities.

Once you've placed the order and paid your 30 percent, production will begin. At this point you should be in regular communication with your supplier rep. You should have already learned the production time, and a good rep will tell you at every stage what's going on with your production. When production is done, it is extremely important for you to feel good about the finished product, because you're on the hook for the remaining 70 percent. I like to have my supplier send me pictures of the boxes and of the box contents. They don't have to send me a picture of the inside of every box, but I do like to have pictures of a couple of them. It's even better if they also send me pictures of the product as soon as it comes off the manufacturing floor before it has been boxed. That way I know my products have been made, they've been looked at and are ready to ship.

Some Minor Housekeeping Notes

A lot of the minutiae about actually setting up accounts and sending in products are freely available on Amazon and so this book doesn't cover those. That said, there are minor things you may overlook that I want to mention. First, make sure you look at packaging requirements for Fulfillment by Amazon (FBA). Amazon has specific standards that they expect to be met and will reject your product if they are not.

For example, liquid products have to either be double sealed or in a polybag. Polybags must have the standard suffocation warning on them. Your products also must have what Amazon calls an FNSKU barcode label on them. You can pay Amazon to apply these for you but they charge $0.20 per unit. You can apply them yourself too if you get the goods shipped to you first. You can also have your logistics team apply them in most cases, but that adds to the labor costs. The most cost-effective way to do it is to either have the barcode integrated with the custom packaging art, or have your supplier apply the labels.

The FNSKU will not be generated until you attempt to create your first shipment within Amazon. However, you won't want to create your shipment until your goods are inside the United States (if they come by sea). So, you'll need to create a fake shipment and cancel it as soon as the FNSKU is generated.

This special barcode also creates a lot of confusion because your products will require a valid UPC or EAN. Yes, you have to have a GS-1 UPC or EAN in order to list a product on Amazon. However, the FNSKU is the barcode that Amazon warehouse workers scan in order to fulfill orders. So for the purposes of selling on Amazon, this barcode takes precedence and you'll need to ensure it's on your products in order for them to be sold on Amazon.

Next Steps

Before placing an order, it is crucial that all your i's are dotted and your t's crossed before making a commitment. You're just learning this process and you'll likely make mistakes along the way. The more prepared you are, however, the easier it will be to overcome them. Here are a few little things you want to consider:

Do the poly bags that your products are packed in have the standard warning and suffocation label on them?

Is your supplier going to print the Amazon FNSKU (barcode) label and put it on your product?

If so, did they print labels on the right paper and in the right size?

Is everything on your packaging spelled correctly?

The best way to make sure that you're fully prepared is to familiarize yourself with all of Amazon's rules about shipping certain products into FBA. Every little detail is important because the last thing you want is to have your shipment turned away at the warehouse. I'm not saying that will happen from a minor mistake but better to be safe than sorry.

Logistics

It's time to talk about one of the most intimidating aspects of importing. Logistics.

How do you actually go about getting your goods from their country of origin over the ocean to you? This particular leg of the journey is fraught with confusion, misunderstandings, and ultimately a lot of fear. This is the part where we worry ourselves to death about customs and all the other things that we don't understand. The good news is it's only really scary the first time.

In order to fully explore this topic, we need to take a step back. The very first thing you must determine is how you plan on shipping the goods. You have two options—air and sea. Air shipments are the fastest but also the most expensive. Sea shipments allow you to bring very large quantities over to the U.S. at a surprisingly affordable rate. They just take much longer and it is a process involving many more steps.

Shipment by Air

Typically most people starting with small first orders will end up shipping by air. Airfreight is not only the fastest way to get your goods but also the easiest. You can get a door-to-door quote and simply have your goods shipped directly to the end destination. Most carriers who handle airfreight will also handle customs but that depends on the product. Most likely you'll be dealing with UPS, FedEx or DHL. Sometimes you'll deal with China Post or other foreign entities, but be aware that these tend to take a lot longer.

You'll have a couple of options regarding how to pay for your air shipment. One of the first questions your supplier will ask you is whether or not you have your own carrier account. At this stage in the game you probably won't. People with carrier accounts usually do a lot of shipping, and over the course of doing that shipping they've negotiated better rates. If you don't have a carrier account chances are you're not going to get the best rates when you open a new account. Usually, it's best to use your supplier's account. Your supplier probably ships things on a regular basis all over the world and that means that they can negotiate the best rates.

Once you've decided what account to use, the type of product you're importing will determine whether or not you're going to get an express quote that handles shipment from the factory to its final destination or if the shipment is only going to be delivered to the port. If your shipment is handled door-to-door then your courier will clear customs for you, and you'll get a bill in the mail or by a phone call for your duties and taxes. This is also referred to as "delivered duty paid," or DDP.

Sometimes the shipment is too large or worth too much money for your supplier to be willing to use their account to set up door-to-door shipment. That means your shipment will be delivered to an airport and no further. From the airport you will be responsible for clearing customs. You can have a customs broker do this or you can do it yourself. I won't go over the details on how to do it yourself, because quite honestly I've never done it, but I know of people who have and I heard that the process really isn't that complicated. It's just a new skill that you have to learn. It involves properly filling out a couple of important pieces of paperwork and paying the right people. After that your goods should arrive at the final destination ready to sell.

Inspecting the Goods

So where is the final destination? This is another important thing to consider. If you're planning to sell these goods on an e-commerce platform like Amazon, the most convenient place to send it is the Amazon warehouse. The only problem with doing it that way is that you don't get a chance to inspect the goods. I recommend that you either have your goods air-shipped to you or to an inspection service first. At least for the first two or three shipments you should definitely have the ability to see what's in the boxes to make sure that it's a quality product. If you did your job right in selecting a supplier, your product should be fine. However, sometimes, even if samples are flawless, the factory cuts corners on the actual mass production and you end up getting an inferior product. That could be the end of your business if you don't find out about the situation until unhappy customers let you know.

However, inspecting in the U.S. may only be necessary if you air ship a fragile item prone to damage in transit. Otherwise, the best way to handle inspection is to have it taken care of in the manufacturing country. If you're having your goods manufactured in China, then I recommend AsiaInspection. This service is specifically for hiring individuals to go to your contracted factory and put your products through a rigorous set of tests. If your products are being manufactured in some other country, it is very likely that they have similar services you can find with a quick search.

Another option is to hire a freelancer to do a less informed and less rigorous but probably less expensive inspection for you. For example, you can either hire someone in the manufacturing country off of a freelancer website like Upwork or place a classified ad on a freelancer site for a manual laborer. This type of inspection isn't particularly sophisticated, but it's very cost-effective. However you choose to obtain this "inspector," you can then send them to the factory to photograph the product and maybe even video Skype you while they tour the factory. It won't be as thorough as an official inspection, but it is a lot less expensive and will give you at least a look at what you're getting.

Taking care of inspection at the factory will help you know that you're getting a quality product. Then you can ship directly to the Amazon warehouse.

Some people prefer to handle inspection themselves once they get the goods. This doesn't save you from stopping subpar goods from being manufactured in the first place, but it will save you from selling any. However you choose to get it done, it is very important that your goods are checked before they're prepped for selling. The next step after that is to make sure that your goods are properly prepped to be sent to the Amazon fulfillment center. This means all boxes must be in good condition and labeled with box labels. If the box is over 150 kilograms, it should be palletized and no more than six feet tall on a standard European dimension pallet. Pallets must be shrink-wrapped and labeled on all four sides with pallet labels as well.

Shipment by Sea

That's as complicated as it gets when it comes to air shipment. Sea shipment is a completely different beast. Sea shipments are, as I mentioned, for much larger shipments. The advantage is that shipments over 250 or 300 pounds become extremely affordable by sea freight as they become unreasonably expensive by air.

Sea shipments are shipped over in containers and all containers have the same weight. That means you're charged more for volume within the container and weight isn't really a factor. Because every 20-foot container weighs a little over 5000 pounds, you could have a shipment of bowling balls, and the weight of those balls really wouldn't affect your rates. How much space in the container your bowling balls are taking up is more important.

When you set up your sea freight you will do so with one of two options. Either LCL, which is less than a container load, or FCL, which is a full container load. Standard containers are 20-footers. However, there are also larger 40-foot containers. Chances are your first sea shipment will be an LCL. That means your goods are sharing the container with other shipments. Keep in mind this adds a little bit of time to your shipping because the container will have to go to a more centralized location and from there be broken apart. Then your portion of the shipment may have extra travel to its final destination.

The best way to ensure that your LCL or FCL shipment makes it to your country is to hire a logistics company. This book will be referring to the United States since that is where I live and sell. Instructions for other countries can be found with a quick internet search. You can use a logistics company that is primarily based out of the United States or you can source a logistics company on a bridge website like Alibaba the same way that you sourced your goods. However, when it comes to this aspect of the process I recommend that you work with someone who fully understands your language and the laws surrounding importing to the United States. It's relatively easy to conduct an internet search to find logistics companies that can handle picking up your goods, putting them in a container and shipping them to the United States. I recommend also making sure that your prospective logistics company offers customs clearance. Rolling these two services into one allows you to have one point of contact that is held accountable for your shipment.

When dealing with sea freight another important thing you must know about is something called Incoterms. Incoterms, or International Commercial Terms, are a series of pre-defined commercial terms published by the International Chamber of Commerce (ICC). That might sound intimidating, but with a little knowledge they are easily handled. An internet search or search on Wikipedia will tell you all you need to know about Incoterms, so we won't spend a lot of time on them here. I just want to touch on a couple of the ones that you're most likely to run into. They involve point of ownership transfer.

Free-On-Board

Most quotes that you'll get from an overseas supplier are what's called FOB, which stands for "free-on-board." FOB is the only way that I import my sea shipments. Free-on-board means the supplier is responsible for all costs associated with getting your goods from the factory, to the port and onto the ship. This includes all loading costs.

The other term that you'll run into is ex works (EXW). Ex works means that you are the one who is responsible for the goods from the moment production is completed. I don't recommend ex works because it can be expensive to have your logistics company arrange shipment from the factory all the way to the port, which may involve laborers traveling from the port through mountainous terrain all the way to the remote area where the factory is located, and from there by truck or train all the way back to the port. That's a lot of involved travel time, and it will also involve export fees that you'll be responsible for under EXW. I definitely recommend FOB.

Insurance

A note about insurance: when you're shipping millions of dollars' worth of inventory every year, you will want to study up on the different types available to you, but in the beginning stages of your business, it's not necessary to dive too deeply into insurance. As you go through the process of getting your product from there to here, you'll likely be offered various policies and you can decide then which ones you want, if any.

Finding a Logistics Company

Now that you've decided on an FOB shipment, you'll want to find a logistics company that offers customs clearance to handle it. That means they are going to send people that they have working in the country of manufacture to the port to meet your factory workers. Together they load the boxes onto the ship and the logistics team sees it all the way to you. I'm going to refer you to BGI Worldwide Logistics, the logistics company I use, but an internet search will bring up other companies you can research and choose from.

Warehouse Distribution Centers

Now the big question. Where should you have your product shipped to? You may consider having it shipped to you. However, chances are your garage isn't big enough to handle a sea shipment worth of goods. Furthermore, unless you live right next to a major port, the shipment will require another mode of transport from the port to you. I recommend having it shipped to a warehouse distribution center. And the reason is because if you're selling your goods on Amazon they require that the goods be palletized, shrink-wrapped and specifically labeled. Rather than take the chance of having your foreign supplier messing up this process, I prefer having the palletization done at a warehouse distribution center in the United States. Aside from that, pallets here are cheaper and the right size.

Where do you find a warehouse distribution center? They're all over the place, but because I'm fond of rolling services all into one, I suggest finding a logistics company that offers customs clearance and either has its own warehouse distribution center or a relationship with a warehouse distribution center. Often these centers have several locations, and you can choose which location you use.

I suggest finding a warehouse distribution center near a port that's close to the manufacturing country. I have my goods manufactured in China and have them shipped to Los Angeles where my warehouse distribution center is. That means my goods are only on the water for 16 days. I live on the East Coast. If I were to have my goods shipped to the East Coast it would take 45 days. That's far too long for me to wait, so I keep that in mind when arranging shipments.

If you don't ship out of China, the thinking remains the same but obviously your specific logistics will vary. Once you've landed upon the best logistics company and distribution center, you've won half the battle of acquiring your product. Now you simply put your rep at the logistics company in touch with your rep from your factory and they will hash out most of the details.

Pro Tip: *Figure out the exact dimensions and weight of your total shipment and then contact as many logistics handlers as you possibly can and get quotes. This will not only allow you to figure out what price is best for your budget, but it will also allow you to test the responsiveness and professionalism of your prospective logistics partner.*

Smooth Shipping Tips

- Make sure that your supplier is aware of all of the important information necessary to properly fill out paperwork. That means they need to know your company's name and address. They need to know that your company is the importer of record and the consignee.

- Keep in mind that the destination is not your company's

address. The destination is your company's contract warehouse run by your freight forwarder.

- Make sure that your supplier prints the necessary information on the outside of the cartons that they send your goods in. Something I learned early is that if there's nothing on the outside of the boxes, customs will always open them to see what's inside. It's important to clearly note on the box what is inside as well as the destination.

- Have your supplier print the commodity on the box, the number of units in the box, the name of your company, the address of the destination (the warehouse distribution center), and the color or other specific variations. The warehouse workers that are palletizing your goods will also have to know this information.

Customs Clearance

After your goods get over the ocean and into the U.S., the next leg of this race is customs clearance. In order to facilitate an error-free customs clearance, it's a good idea for you to be the one to identify your tariff code or HS code ahead of time. The customs broker on your logistics team can do this as well, but they are not infallible and may not do it properly. It's best for you to figure out what your own HS code is. The HS code (sometimes also referred to as HTS code) is the number that identifies what your commodity is and the duty rate, or tariff, that you will pay. Typically this takes some research to find out. There are websites that are specifically designed to locate HS codes, but most of them cost money. To get the information for free you have to do a little digging. Unfortunately, it's not as easy as searching for the HS code for such-and-such blue widgets. A lot of what determines the HS code for a commodity is what it is made of and used for. Garlic presses, for example, might be stainless steel and cooking. Pretty simple. It can get more complicated, however, if you sell a plastic, not a metal, bottle opener that also has the ability to open other things.

The easiest way to correctly identify your product is to search for what you think might describe it best, and then look up similar companies with similar products to see what codes they have been imported with. This will help you be more certain about your tariff notice. You can simply supply that information to your customs broker. Usually they'll be thankful because you just did the hard part for them and they'll import your product under that code. In some cases they might disagree, but if you did your research right that won't happen. You can find all this information by doing a lot of Googling.

Once the HS code is identified then your customs broker will clear customs for you. During this process a lot of different things can happen, and it's best not to be surprised by any of them. Ideally a couple days after you give your broker the go-ahead, you'll get an email saying that your goods have been cleared. Be aware that occasionally your container may be set aside for X-ray examination. This is especially true for new shipments. This isn't that big of a deal, but it does add three or four days to the waiting process and costs you a little extra money. Some containers are set aside for full inspection, and this is probably the worst case scenario. Full inspection means that customs will open every single carton inside the container. This can prolong the clearance process anywhere from two weeks to even longer, and unfortunately the cost to you is pretty substantial.

I don't tell you that to scare you away but to make you aware that any of those scenarios could happen when you import. You simply have to be prepared and go with the flow. When your goods finally get cleared out of customs, if you set everything up right your logistics company should then take your goods and deliver them to a warehouse. After the warehouse has communicated with you how long it will take them to put everything on pallets, you can create shipments within Amazon. With Amazon you have access to their partnered LCL carriers and will pay a very discounted rate to have their trucks come to your warehouse and pick up your goods. Alternately you can have your own trucking company, or your logistics companies, take your goods from the warehouse to the fulfillment center. For the seasoned entrepreneur, your warehouse distribution center might also be your fulfillment center, and then that step can be ignored entirely.

At this point all aspects of logistics are over except for the bill you'll be getting to pay for all of those services. Don't worry, you'll have gotten estimates of these costs and there should be no surprises. Now you can focus on what's important, which is selling and growing your brand.

Important Side Note: You can actually have your goods confiscated by customs for a couple of reasons. One is importing counterfeits. It should go without saying that you do not want to do this. Another is not having your goods labeled with the country of origin. If you forget this important step, customs will have you come to their office and label each item yourself (if they're nice).

Next Steps

You have just been given a lot of really dense information about how to get your goods from there to here. It's a lot to think about but with a little planning you can increase your chances for a smooth import. Below are a few questions to get you started.

Will you ship by air or sea? Why?

How will you handle inspection?

If you're shipping by sea will you be shipping FOB or EXW? (FOB is recommended.)

Where will you have your goods shipped?
    Port:
    Warehouse:
    Fulfillment: (most likely Amazon)

What is your product's HS code?

Part Four:

The Listing

Creating the Listing

Now that you've found a great product, found a supplier, negotiated the deal and imported the product, it's time to start making some money. You can sell your items on eBay, Sears.com, Rakuten, and even on your own website. However, this book will walk you through selling specifically on Amazon. We won't go over the specifics on how to set up an account, because that information is freely available on Amazon's website, but I will go over some of the options you'll encounter. First, I would recommend that you use Fulfillment by Amazon (FBA). This is where Amazon acts as your fulfillment center, and takes care of the warehousing and distribution of your product when orders are placed. Your other option is to fulfill the product yourself, which is referred to as "fulfillment by merchant." You will need your own fulfillment house and warehousing in order to do that. Or, you can fulfill orders out of your own home. When you set up an account you also have the option of either choosing a personal account or a professional account. A professional account costs $40 a month. A personal account is free, but you will be charged one dollar for every item you sell. If you utilize the launching methods that I recommend in the next section, you will sell far more than 40 items in your first month, so I recommend the professional account.

When you have your account set up, the next thing that you will need to do on Amazon is set up your listing. Every product sold on Amazon has a listing, which is basically the display page, sales copy and images for the product on Amazon's catalog. This is where buyers will find pictures and descriptive copy explaining exactly what your product is and how they can purchase it. The Amazon listing is one of the most important parts of your business. How you present your brand and product with photography and sales copy makes the difference between product sales or a product flop. On top of all of that, your listing will also need to contain important keywords so Amazon's search algorithm will be able to properly find and place your product in a competitive spot in search rankings.

Know that Amazon requires you to create your account and listings before you can ship your items into Amazon's warehouses. There are two ways to add products to Amazon's catalog. The most common and easiest way is to add them one by one in the inventory management area of seller central. The second way is to upload a flat file. I will explain in detail how to do both. Understand that the reason the flat file option exists is primarily for people with many different items to sell. In my experience, however, adding your products one by one is much easier and often less time consuming as it is less technical.

Now let's take a close look at and break down exactly what makes an optimal listing.

The Title

Here is a super technical outline of a proper title:

[Brand] + [Feature] + [Product Type] + [Model Number/Type] + [Size] + [Package Count] + [Color] + [Scent] + [Flavor]*

*(According to Amazon's terms)

It looks funny out of context, so I'll explain it all step-by-step. Depending on the product, you'll adjust the variables of this formula accordingly. For instance, an iPhone case doesn't have a scent so you would leave this field blank.

Keep in mind that a title is a third of the reason consumers will click on your listing. Photos and price make up the rest of the equation. The title is your opener on any sales page. It must draw the buyer's attention, and invoke the "I need this" feeling. It has to offer an undeniable benefit, preferably one that isn't over-used by the competition. It's also a good idea to add other details that build value for your product (like a nanostructured coating on a screen protector).

The key to all of this is making your title readable with clear benefits while also incorporating keywords that allow Amazon's algorithm to rank your listing.

Remember, inadvertently slowing down the consumer with a badly worded title as they try to decipher if your product is right for them will cause them to quickly lose interest and move on.

First, let's take a moment to think about your brand. For some, branding is extremely important. If you plan to extend your branding over multiple offerings, you'll want to be certain that your brand is used in your title, especially if you offer a specific line of products.

If you're offering a single product that is one of many unconnected products, branding may not be essential. Make this choice, and either build your brand name by stamping it proudly in the title of every listing, or leave space for some extra keywords. That choice is up to you and where you want to see your brand go. It is important to note, however, that in extensive research of hundreds of listings on Amazon, it was found that in many categories the majority of page one listings included a brand name in the title.

No matter what your intentions may be for the future of your particular brand, letting people know who you are is a critical part of the process, and the title is the place to start doing that. Don't just slap something in the title that everyone else is doing, because then you will just melt into the crowd, and you *do not* want to do that. You have to make the product unique; give it an allure through your proven, unique features, and the little voice in your potential buyers' heads will say, "You may want to take a closer look at this one."

Be sure to clearly state your product. Don't muddle it. It's important that the consumer can see what they're getting right away. It's also important to get to this part as quickly as possible. In different browser windows, on various devices, Amazon's search results pages will truncate the title. If your title gets cut off before it explains what you have to offer, you lose out on clarity that could help you land a sale.

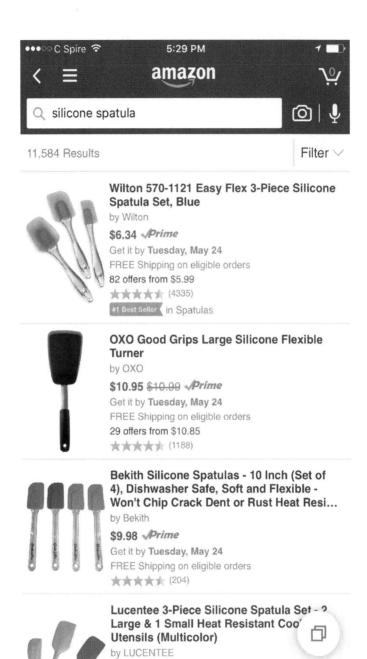

Figure 4-1: Examples of descriptive titles.

One suggestion Amazon makes is to state things like color or size in the title (see Figure 4-1). The reason for this is to ensure that a potential buyer, searching for a specific item, can locate your product if it fits their needs. Another reason is because sizes and colors (or various other features) often are included in heavily searched terms.

Most importantly, the title should sell the product. Even though Amazon would like titles to be on the purely informational side of things, there is still room here to make your keyword combinations enticing, and it's important that you take the time to do so. So many sellers make the mistake of having a poor title. Customers take note if a seller looks like they care about what they're doing. You should consider your title a representation of your product and your business.

That means the title should be to the point and concise but appealing. Super long, spammy titles are not only no longer allowed, but are unattractive to most buyers.

In the process of constructing this title, make absolutely sure that you're hitting your major keywords! (We'll talk more about keyword research later on.) Use high-ranking, niche specific keywords in your title for better results, and if you can't fit them all, that's what the back end "Search Terms" section is for. The key to using keywords correctly comes down to effective keyword research and making sure you are using the best ones.

Avoid superfluous words like "premium" and "first-class" unless you're just trying to fill space (which is something you usually won't do if you've done your keyword research right). Also, don't try to overstuff your title with keywords. You can try to put together exact match keyword phrases, but if they don't sound natural, it isn't necessary. Amazon's algorithm is intelligent enough to stitch individual words into key phrases for you.

To illustrate all this in action, let's look at a few examples. Let's say you sell a pet deshedding tool. There are many keywords you may wish to target for such a tool: deshedder, shedding brush, shed rake, deshedding tool, pet grooming tool, long haired dog brush, etc. The list goes on. If you tried to cram all of that into your title, it is going to look bad and likely be against Amazon's new

Term of Service (TOS).

Here is an example of a concise title for this product:

Paw Pals 2 in 1 Deshedding Tool w/ Shed Blade & Rake - Shedding Brush for Dogs & Cats of All Sizes & Fur Length - Hair Remover to Alleviate Allergies by Reducing 95% Dander & Undercoat - Quality Pet Grooming Supplies

This is a real title that complies with Amazon's 200 character limit. Aspects of it were actually originally changed to meet Amazon's specific rules (they made us move the brand to the front of the title). This title ranks for many keywords:

- deshedding tool

- shed blade

- shed rake

- shedding brush for dogs

- shedding brush for cats

- hair remover

- cat dander

- pet grooming supplies

- pet grooming tools

Notice it also conveys the benefits of removing undercoat and reducing dander to alleviate allergies (and being 2 in 1).

Now that was a much longer example, but here is one that shows you can have quite an impact even with a short title:

Pure Antarctic Krill Oil - Omega 3 Fatty Acids Supplement Packed w/ DHA & EPA - Natural Anti Inflammatory & Antioxidant w/ Choline & Astaxanthin

This one doesn't focus on the brand so much, but is extremely concise with the offer. It also uses big keywords like omega 3, omega fatty acids, omega 3 supplement, DHA, EPA, anti inflammatory, antioxidant, choline and astaxanthin. The title conveys the benefit of being "packed" with DHA and EPA as well as other commonly searched ingredients. We also have room to add pill count if we choose (pill count matters in certain niches and not in others).

Just like an algebraic formula, you can move some of the elements around and still have the desired result. For example, sometimes you might want to add the brand to the end, such as "Quality Kitchen Accessories by KitchenAwesome." Just remember to be direct, honest and create value with your title, and you are well on your way to making a sale.

Next Steps

Fill in all the details that pertain to your product:

Brand:

Feature:

Product Type:

Model Number/Type:

Size:

Package:

Count:

Color:

Scent:

Flavor:

String the terms together in order of most important to least important to create your title.

Title:

Photos

The next thing that we need to discuss is photography. Your photos are the single most important element of your listing, whether that be on Amazon or any other e-commerce platform. In search results, the thumbnail of the main image is the main attraction for your potential buyer. It's what catches the eye during those unfocused browsing moments of search before a purchase is made. After they click on your listing, buyers will see the rest of your photos and those should tell the story of what it is you have to offer.

It cannot be stressed enough how important it is to not cut corners on the photography. In fact, the biggest portion of your initial investment in marketing should go toward photography. Regardless of how big or small your budget is, you need to find the most professional, talented and experienced photographer (or photographers) who can provide you with the best photographs possible. If you cut corners on this step, it will be a very expensive mistake.

When looking for a photographer, you are looking for someone who has experience with catalog photography. These are going to be the stunningly crisp, clean pictures of your product (and only your product) on a white background, as required by Amazon (see Figure 4-2). Their terms also state that you can't use effects, but they're pretty lax when it comes to enforcing that, so a drop shadow or a slight reflection underneath your product might be a nice touch—something that looks classy, yet still grabs attention. The way you will determine whether or not your photographer has the ability to offer this is to look at their portfolio. Ideally they will have experience taking pictures of products that are much like yours.

Figure 4-2: Catalog photograph of a product on a white background.

A lot of listings on Amazon only feature these product-only types of photographs. However, you're missing out on telling the story of your product and your brand if you stick to this route. Another important elements of your photography should be action or staged shots. These are pictures that show your product either in use or with the elements necessary to operate it. For example, if you sell an iPhone dock, you'll want to include an image of your dock being used with an iPhone (see Figure 4-3). Or if you sell a garlic press, you may want to have either a picture of your garlic press in the middle of pressing garlic or, at the very least, a nice staged shot of the garlic press, with some garlic cloves sitting right next to it, conveying the purpose of your product. If you sell kitchen knives, pictures with sliced vegetables on a cutting board are essential. These staged shots offer a backdrop or setting that gives your product listing more color and relevance.

Figure 4-3: iPhone photographed in a dock with an accessory.

Action shots show your product actually being used by a person and give you the opportunity to depict your target demographic. For example, if you sell a product primarily to men in their 40s, then show a man in his 40s using the product. If the main buyers of your yoga mats are stay-at-home moms, then your yoga mat listing should have a picture of a woman in her early 30s in tree pose on your yoga mat. If you sell an arthritis cream, then having a picture of the senior rubbing a cream into their joints is a good way to go.

This imagery does the best job at actually selling your product. Most of the time you cannot use it as your main image, because that's against Amazon's terms of service. However, these photos will do their job of converting the buyer once they make it to your listing. The reason these photos work so well is they allow the buyers to picture themselves using your product.

Figure 4-4: Image of target demographic using a product.

If you sell a consumable, you may have to get a little creative when it comes to staged and action shots. Including images of your ingredients is one way to go. Also remember that a very important aspect of consumables listings is clear shots of the ingredients and the directions.

Pro Tip: *Make sure that your images are very high resolution. I like mine to be at minimum 1500 x 1500 pixels. That way the potential buyer can expand the photograph and read any instructions, directions or other information (and it just looks better).*

You may also want to consider using infographics. Amazon has some vague terms that most people interpret to mean they don't want wording in the images. However, upon careful examination it appears that you are allowed to have words in your images as long as they're not in your main image, and the product is at least 80 percent of the photo (see Figure 4-5). This gives you a small amount of room to use wording to help convey deeper information about your product. If you have a particularly technical product or if your product has a lot of features, an infographic can be very helpful. You might be able to design one yourself, or you might want to hire a graphic designer to help you with the design work.

Figure 4-5: Infographic displaying product features.

Ideally, you'll be able to get all of these images taken care of by the same photographer. However, you may find that your photographer specializes in one area and not the other. In my own experience I've seen that photographers who take catalog shots on a white background do a great job doing just that, but may not be the best at taking action shots. And photographers who take fantastic pictures of people in motion and products in action might lack the proper setup to take catalog pictures.

Also keep in mind that action shots will require models. This is where photography can get a little expensive. Again, I stress that it is well worth it. The reason is because your biggest competitors are big brands. Big, multi-million-dollar brands have extremely professional photography. That photography is complete with well-done infographics, carefully selected models, and gorgeous catalog photography. It's best to start out in the same way rather than lose sales to the big players because you didn't put enough money and effort into your product shots. But no matter how many photographers you have to hire, or how many models you have to get involved, it is essential that this be where your focus is in the beginning.

Next Steps

Research commercial photographers in your area. Find photographers who specialize in still/product photography as well as action shots. Call and get quotes for at least three. Take notes when you call about any specifications or extra services they might offer.

Photographer #1:

Photographer #2:

Photographer #3:

Keywords

The next element of your Amazon product listing will be your keywords. Before you even started writing you should have completed substantial keyword research. Keywords are essential because these are the words that will determine where your product is ranked in a search. It is only through identifying the most profitable keywords that you will understand where you need to focus your marketing so you can make the most money.

Your keyword research will affect how you write your title. It will also affect how you write the rest of your listing. Back-end search term keywords are just as important to ranking as the title. Amazon uses these keywords by identifying the ones that are relevant and then, over time, combines each and every one of them into key terms and phrases. Then Amazon will index your product on search pages for every one of those key terms. Everything on Amazon, at least as far as the algorithm is concerned, operates on keywords. Each word is put into a number of combinations with other words. As those search terms result in sales, your product will rank higher for each one. This is why as a product builds up a large catalog of "long tail key phrases" it can become more profitable over time.

You want to use every possible bit of real estate in your search term back-end keywords section. Don't use any commas and don't repeat any words. Try to put the keywords into logical key phrases. Even doing this it may still look like a garbled mess of words, but that means you did right. You simply take the most relevant keywords, and any keywords that are related to those, and add them to the five lines that you have in the search terms section of your listing. List as many relevant words as you can, with nothing but a space between them.

This is where you'll put words such as "for men, women, gift, present." Keep in mind, this is not an exact science, and often times you will find yourself tweaking this section, in conjunction with tweaking your title, to get your product to rank for certain terms. The reason for that is because Amazon's complex algorithm first and foremost searches for relevance. Sometimes even the most obvious terms located in your keyword section will not register as relevant, and they must be considered relevant if you want to have impressions in your sponsor product ads, or any rankings for those keywords. I mention that just to drive home the point that this is not a static thing. The most successful listings are the ones that can adapt to changes in the market, changes in the algorithm, changes in direction, and all the other changes this business may throw your way.

Keyword Research

There are a couple of good strategies for conducting keyword research. The first one I'd like to suggest is a program called MerchantWords, which serves up search volume specifically for keywords used in Amazon search. MerchantWords is not infallible. Sometimes it can be inaccurate. But it is the most reliable resource for getting a general idea of the search volume specific keywords receive on Amazon that I have found. No matter what other tools you use, I advise that you also use MerchantWords.

Google Keyword Planner is also important. Keyword Planner has been around a long time and is used to search for keywords relevant for Google. Understand that Google and Amazon will always be very different platforms, especially in regards to keyword searches, primarily because Google searches are for information and Amazon searches are for purchases. However, high-volume search terms in Google that also translate to high-volume search terms in Amazon are typically the types of winners you are looking for.

Google Trends is also a good tool. Google Trends allows you to see whether or not an important search term correlates to a growing search trend. This will give you an idea as to whether or not the market you're planning on going into is expanding and gaining more interest. Aside from being a keyword tool, Google

Trends is also a great product research tool.

Amazon's built in auto-suggestion is also valuable and easy to use. You type in a keyword in the search box of Amazon, and you'll see that it automatically brings up a number of suggestions as to what the rest of that search phrase should be (see Figure 4-6). This gives you an idea of what other people are searching for. You can do it term by term, or get another program to do it for you. Either way, it is valuable information to see what Amazon's own algorithm will suggest as far as keywords are concerned.

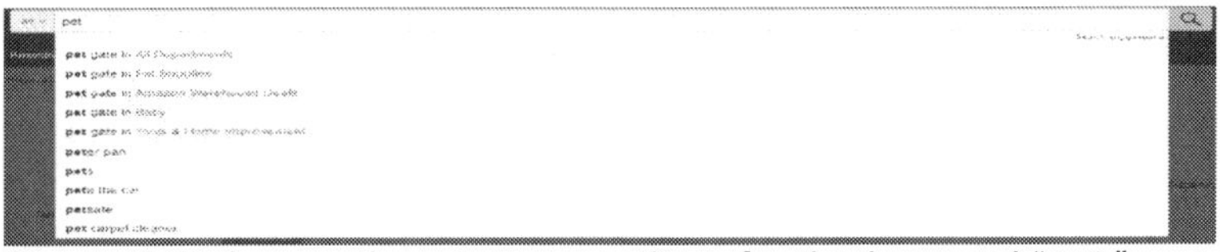

Figure 4-6: Amazon's auto-suggestions for the keyword "pet."

If you're struggling to figure out what types of keywords you should be using or targeting, a good idea is to look at the keywords your competitors are using. The simplest way to do this is by analyzing their listings. Another way is to use a program called Simple Keyword Inspector and do what they refer to as a reverse ASIN search. The program essentially scrapes the listing and serves up to you all the keywords that the listing ranks for. If your competitor has a website, you can also include that in a Keyword Planner search. Google's Keyword Planner allows you to search specific terms, phrases or websites. So by putting in your competitor's website and running a search, Google will provide you with all of the relevant search terms found from that website.

With all of these tools available to you, you should have no trouble finding more keywords than you'll know what to do with. The important thing is to find the keywords that are going to lead to the most sales. Use these tools as a starting point, but refine your approach by using Amazon itself. The best way to do that is in the form of sponsored product ads. By running an "automatic campaign" you'll be able to identify the keywords that actually convert to sales. This strategy is a little bit complex, and I promise to give you more in-depth information when we reach the section about paid advertising.

Next Steps

Using as many of the research tools as your budget can afford, come up with the most comprehensive keyword and phrase list possible. Don't worry about repeating words for now. List keywords that have the highest search volume first. These are the words you'll use in your title and listing. You can use the rest of the terms on the back end.

High search volume keywords:

Keywords on the Back End (Search Terms)

Now, let's dig a little deeper into the back end. Remember: *no commas and no repeating words*. The back end is designed to be a catch all for those great keywords that just didn't have a place in your title (but you'll want to include your title keywords here as well). For example, say your product was that deshedding brush for dogs. If you had key phrases left over like pet grooming tools, pet grooming equipment, pet grooming supplies and pet supplies for dogs, you'd break these down in the back end like this:

pet grooming tools equipment supplies for dogs

Notice how there are no commas and no repeating words. This is just an example, but it applies to any list of keywords. The more relevant keywords you can put in your search terms field, the better. Make sure they are relevant and are parts of a keyword or key phrase that ranks well, as they are very important to the search algorithm.

In conclusion, think of the title first. The title is so important to the life of your listing. Keep it interesting, and keep it full of relevant keywords. Then be sure to keep your back end updated and viable, and you absolutely will start ranking better. If you don't think you have it quite right, don't be afraid to make adjustments. Do keep in mind, though, that adjustments may initially cause you to drop ranking while the algorithm adjusts. However, if you have made real improvements on your front-end and back-end keyword setup, you'll see yourself regain traction quickly and eventually see improvement in your rankings.

A Note on Testing

I've mentioned several times that you want to constantly change and evolve your listing to ensure the freshest and most optimized approach. This is called "testing." It isn't something that you do whimsically or without forethought either. Testing should be methodical and strategic.

When testing elements of your listing, be sure to do it in small chunks and allow enough time to elapse to get good data. So, start with, for example, the title. Change ONLY the title and let that sit for about a week and see if that results in a positive impact on ranking or conversion. If it does, then move on to the next element. If it doesn't, change it back. Then test something else (like the main image, bullets or search terms).

Next Steps

Go back to the keyword list you made during your research and strike all the repeating words. You now have your keywords for the back end of your product listing.

Bullets

Every listing on Amazon has a section known as the bullet points (see Figure 4-7). These are the lines around the middle of the listing that outline the product features and benefits. Bullets are indexed for search terms, but are nowhere near as important as keywords and titles. In my own testing, I've seen very little impact in regard to search rank when it comes to bullets.

About the Product
- EXTENDS WAIST STRAP - Works for all 3 button Mo+m Carrier waist strap buckles
- ADDS NEEDED BREATHING ROOM - Adds 9 inches around the waist
- BABY WEARERS OF ALL SIZES - Now everyone in the family can enjoy baby wearing, no matter what size they are

See more product details

Figure 4-7: Bullet points outlining features and benefits of the product.

The most important thing about bullets is the overview of benefits they give to your potential buyer. Bullets represent a powerful potential to sway a buyer and thereby gain a sale and increase your conversion rate. Prevailing wisdom might suggest that having powerful, keyword rich copy in this section is the best way to go. While I agree with that, I also think that it's very important to keep this section as brief and concise as possible.

It's tempting to look at the bullets as a way to fill your listing with tons of great sales copy. The problem with this is most people aren't going to read walls of text in your bullets. If you keep the information concise, only outlining the best benefits to your buyer, you will see the power of your bullets in increasing conversions.

This bulleted section probably will evolve over time, because as you sell you will start seeing patterns in what people like and don't like about your product. When you discover the features that excite most buyers, you can use those as your first bullets. It will eventually become clear that other features aren't so important and you can drop those to the bottom of the list or remove them entirely.

Pro Tip: *In the beginning, before you have customer data to pull from, mine your competitors' negative reviews and identify features that your product possesses that address those issues. Use these as bullet points.*

Try to keep each bullet to only one line apiece. This will allow all of your bullets to be shown "above the fold," or otherwise on the first page without the need for scrolling down, in Amazon's new layout. Amazon recently changed the layout of listings and on many browsers they actually cut off or truncate most of the bullets. So keep this in mind when creating your listing, as you want all of the most important and relevant information about your product to be easily seen.

Amazon's terms of service do not allow special characters anywhere in your listing. This does keep cheesy and spammy looking symbols and styling off the listings, but it can also make bullets and descriptions look like boring, nondescript walls of text. So, a format that I have used is create a "title" in all capitalized letters, outlining the general idea, and then summarize the benefits after a hyphen.

Next Steps

To come up with your bullet points, list the benefits of using your product in clear, descriptive terms. Remember, only one line each.

1.

2.

3.

4.

5.

Product Description

It is widely speculated whether or not the product description has any bearing on a search. In my experience it has very little impact. Furthermore, it's very likely that many people do not make it all the way down to the product description. Be that as it may, it still behooves you to put information in the product description because this section is indexed for search by Google. Also, if you post a link to your listing on a social media site like Facebook, the description is the area where a snippet preview will be pulled from.

The information that you want to include can vary from technical specs, to sales copy, to accolades. In all of my testing, I really haven't seen any specific format for the product description make a difference in conversion.

One thing I advise, however, is to make the description highly readable. For that reason we use <p> and <b> tags. These are HTML tags for paragraph and bolding. Currently you cannot save changes to your listing if HTML tags are present with the exception of only these two (and in some categories, even these aren't allowed). Some people have still found that they are unable to make changes to their listing if any HTML whatsoever is in it. But in most cases <p> and <b> tags will make it through. These tags are very simple. They don't make anything flashy, and they don't insert anything "black hat" into your listing. All they do is break up the text. I use them to make a bold subhead, followed by paragraph tags to break up specific points that I want to include in the description.

Once you've put the listing together you are ready for your product launch. You're only one section away from watching the money flow into your bank account!

Examples of Product Descriptions

THE IN-LAWS ARE COMING...AND THE HOUSE IS A WRECK
Not because you don't clean it. But because you have some serious shed monsters constantly depositing fresh beds of fur all over your furniture/clothes/bedding and anything else they can get their paws on.

GETTING THIS PLACE TIDY IN TIME MIGHT TAKE A MIRACLE
Or maybe it'll just take a Paw Pals Pet Deshedding Tool (and a vacuum...you know, for the stuff already on the furniture). By regularly using the deshedder, you reduce the amount of fur those little rascals can leave everywhere by a significant amount. Say goodbye to wads of pet hair all over the place and rest easy knowing your home is presentable again.

AND AUNT SALLY CAN FINALLY BREATHE EASY AGAIN
Stop submitting friends and family that are allergic to dander and total torture. Cut down on the shed fur and you won't have to watch people's faces swell uncomfortably every time they try to sit on your couch.

WHAT ARE YOU WAITING FOR?
Click the "Add to Cart" button now and relieve your home of the constant pet fur tornado. You'll also be paving the way for a shinier and healthier coat on your pet. It's a win-win for everyone. And with our We're Pals guarantee, it's also risk free.

   Pro Tip: *Here's what that description looks like before copying and pasting it into the product description section:*

<p><b>THE IN-LAWS ARE COMING....AND THE HOUSE IS A WRECK</b></p>

<p>Not because you don't clean it. But because you have some serious shed monsters constantly depositing fresh beds of fur all over your furniture/clothes/bedding and anything else they can get their paws on.</p>

\<p>\GETTING THIS PLACE TIDY IN TIME MIGHT TAKE A MIRACLE\\</p>

\<p>Or maybe it'll just take a Paw Pals Pet Deshedding Tool (and a vacuum...you know, for the stuff already on the furniture). By regularly using the deshedder, you reduce the amount of fur those little rascals can leave everywhere by a significant amount. Say goodbye to wads of pet hair all over the place and rest easy knowing your home is presentable again.\</p>

\<p>\AND AUNT SALLY CAN FINALLY BREATHE EASY AGAIN\\</p>

\<p>Stop submitting friends and family that are allergic to dander to total torture. Cut down on the shed fur and you won't have to watch people's faces swell uncomfortably every time they try to sit on your couch.\</p>

\<p>\WHAT ARE YOU WAITING FOR?\\</p>

\<p>Click the Add to Cart button now and relieve your home of the constant pet fur tornado. You'll also be paving the way for a shinier and healthier coat on your pet. It's a win-win for everyone. And with our We're Pals guarantee, it's also risk free.\</p>

You can easily create this yourself by going to a free online WYSIWYG editor (such as http://bestonlinehtmleditor.com/) and just typing in your description, using bold and spacing like you would a word document. Then click the "source" button and grab your HTML code.

Next Steps

Using the tips we just discussed, write your product description. You can highlight benefits, tell a story, or list technical specifications here. The goal is to make it look professional and give more pertinent information to your potential customer. For formatting help, you can simply create your listing in a free online WYSIWYG editor. Remember to ONLY use paragraph spacing and bolding.

Pricing

This is such an important factor in your listing. Price is, arguably, one of the top factors in a potential buyer's decision making process. So how do you come up with the best price for your product? You start by evaluating your competitors' prices. This gives you a baseline. Look at similar products in the market and attempt to compare your product to the closest matching value out there. Look at the range from low to high to get an idea of your options.

The next deciding factor is your profit margin. The price of your product should be what your product is worth to the marketplace. However, your profit margin will dictate whether or not you can survive offering your product for those prices.

Many people who look to import from overseas will become star struck and enamored by the seemingly humongous profit margins. You may walk away from a deal convinced you'll have 60 to 80 percent margins. While sometimes this is possible, you must understand there's a good chance reality will not allow this. Often times we believe we can get away with charging premium prices because our competition does. But what we don't pay attention to is the fact that a lot of the competition consists of extremely well established and big brands. You may find it difficult to sell at those premium prices.

That is not to say premium pricing doesn't work for private label products, but it's best to be realistic. Also you must account for changes in the marketplace. You may get away with charging a mint and making 60 percent margins for a long time and then all of a sudden find yourself in a marketplace flooded with competition. While you're floundering to keep your head above water you may discover that lowering your price is the only option.

So definitely go for those high margins, but only so you have room to adapt to the marketplace. Also keep in mind that many businesses run on razor thin margins. These margins can be anywhere from 5 to 15 percent. So if you can walk away with at least 25 percent, that is still a return on your investment. Ideally you'll fall somewhere between 35 and 45 percent or more, however.

The other major thing that price affects on the Amazon marketplace is conversion rate. You may find your product does not convert very well at all at one price, but then find your conversion rate doubles, triples or even quadruples with a lower price. Your price could literally mean the difference between six sales a day and 50. That is why finding the right price is crucial.

But again, how do you do that? In my experience, I like to find a range that represents between 30 and 55 percent profit margins (if I have that range to move in). This represents my rock-bottom price all the way up to my ideal price. My ideal price is on the higher, premium end where a lot of my big brand competitors are. This is the very top of what the quality of my product can command. The bottom is the absolute lowest I feel comfortable going and represents enough profit to make me feel like the effort I'm putting into sourcing and selling the product is worth it.

Typically, when I come into a market with a new product, I'll choose a mid-range price, usually at the lower end of that mid-range so it looks really attractive and extremely valuable compared to my competitors. I'll enter the market at that price and do all of my promotions. I want to make the deal look as attractive as possible to people who are willing to take a chance on a brand-new brand. After my product has gained traction and is seeing a comfortable number of sales every day, I'll start raising the price a dollar or two every couple of days. I continue to do this until my sales drop significantly. This usually means I've found the peak of what the market is willing to pay for my product.

The coolest part about price is that it's really easy to change. So whenever your brand becomes more established and larger, you can play this game again on the premium tier. But for now you want to keep a profitable yet high-value offer to gain as much traction as possible, always keeping in mind that there is a lower tier that you can move to if the marketplace forces you there.

Just remember that your goal should be to grow your brand and your company, but don't get greedy. All too often this is what happens and it stagnates businesses.

Next Steps

Time to figure out your best starting price. Go back to your research about your competitors in Part 3 to answer the next couple of questions:

What is your competitor's price range from low to high?

Choose a price that is around the lower end of mid-range. This is your starting price.

Add up everything it cost you to deliver your product to fulfillment including packaging, shipping, transportation, inspection, customs, warehousing, and cost of goods, and any other fees you incurred along the way.

Divide this number by the total number of units ordered. This is your operating cost per item._____

Calculate 30 percent of your starting price. This is Amazon's approximate cut (referral fee + pick and pack + weight handling. You can also get a more accurate idea by looking up the FBA fee calculator)._____

Now subtract the operating cost and Amazon's cut from the starting price. This is your profit per item._____

Divide your profit by starting price. This is your profit margin. Is it between 35 and 45 percent? If not, adjust your price until you find a profit margin you're comfortable with.

Part Five:

Launching Your Product

The Anatomy of a Product Launch

When you're selling on Amazon's marketplace, your goal is the same as everyone else's—take advantage of the massive traffic of ready-to-purchase buyers who browse Amazon daily looking for products. That is the dream, but in order to live that dream you have to take your product out of obscurity and put it in front of eyeballs. Amazon is a huge and heavily trafficked marketplace, but it is also just a really big catalog. That means without any effort, any product you list in it will be somewhere on the last page, buried under thousands of competitors, with no way for a buyer to find it except to click on the next page into seeming infinity.

That is why you need a product launch. Similar to throwing a grand opening at a physical retail store in hopes of gaining word-of-mouth advertising, a proper product launch secures the most valuable thing you could ever gain in e-commerce: *Momentum*. Product launches on Amazon, however, aren't limited to new products, nor are they a one-time thing. Launching really is just another word for an extremely effective way to promote and grow your brand, and you'll likely take advantage of the process multiple times throughout the life of your business.

Launching a product on Amazon comes down to an equation that needs only slight tweaks to fit your specific situation. It is more science than art, because anyone (and I do mean anyone) can replicate it and see success in virtually all categories on Amazon.

So what is this equation? It's simple arithmetic.

Sales Velocity + Keywords = Ranking

And ideally...

Ranking = Sales

Now let me explain all that a little more.

Sales velocity is the rate at which you get sales over time. So, how can you get more sales if sales are what you're lacking and attempting to get in the first place? Sounds a bit tricky, but we'll get to that in a minute.

Keywords are very important as well, as we've already discussed. Keywords in the URL, search field, title, and search terms help Amazon rank your product in a search. Basically, Amazon's algorithm attempts to serve up the most relevant products in a given search, and relevancy is based on listing optimization as well as popularity. The more people who search for a term and decide *your* product is the one they want, the higher up the rank your listing will go for that keyword.

Ranking = Sales. As I explained earlier, Amazon is a catalog. It also has a very complex and efficient search engine that helps people navigate the catalog. That is how many consumers find the products they wish to buy. Amazon is known for having competitive offers, so rather than seeking out a specific brand, most people type in what they want in the search bar and choose from the array of options presented to them. They are most likely to choose from the ones that are displayed first. But here we go again. If a higher rank is what you need to get sales, how do you make a bunch of sales through a keyword to get a higher rank?

This is where the many launch strategies come into play, and you want to use more than just one. You may choose to build a community around your brand, build an email list of your own, rent someone else's email list, or use paid advertising. You may choose to run heavy discounts, or limited-time promotional pricing or other incentives. No matter what strategy you choose to employ, as long as you approach it with the same goal in mind, you should see success.

For brand-new products, that goal should be sales velocity and reviews. Any way you can, you need to get as many sales as quickly as possible and as many reviews as possible. The most common first step in a launch is to approach friends and family. People that you know often will be more than willing to provide you with the initial reviews and sales that your product listing needs. After that you want to target the largest list of buyers possible and elicit as many sales as you can. The most effective way to do this is to offer buyers your product at a massive discount. The steeper the discount, the more likely the sales velocity will shoot up. And the more products you're able to put into people's hands, the more reviews you'll get. However, we are not advocating giving away or discounting products in exchange for a review as that is against Amazon's terms of service.

And again, there are many different ways to gather that list of buyers. You can work to build your own list through your social media channels or your website. You can use paid advertising to grow a list on either social media or Google. Or you can use a service that effectively gives you access to a list of buyers that they have accrued. You can go on forever researching different launch strategies, but luckily you don't have to. In the rest of this section you'll get an in-depth look into the strategies that I've used time and time again, that *work*! I suggest you use them all together because, as you'll see, they build on one another in order to lift you to the highest level of success with the ranking, reviews and sales you want to push your business to the next level. But first...

Conversion Is the Name of the Game

In my experience, the single most important factor in ranking (aside from the actual sales velocity to a keyword that gets you there) is conversion rate. But what *is* conversion rate? It is the percentage of people who buy your product after visiting your listing.

Amazon's algorithm ranks listings for keywords based on relevancy, and determines relevancy based on popularity, and determines popularity based on conversion rate. The higher your conversion rate, the more popular and relevant for a term your listing will appear, and that, coupled with good sales volume, will push you to the top of the searches.

But how do you increase your conversion rates? The biggest aspect of conversion that you have total control over is the optimization of your listing. The beautiful images, concise but benefit-driven bullets and informative descriptions we discussed earlier are big factors.

Another big factor is social proof, illustrated on Amazon as product reviews. Reviews actually do *not* directly impact search ranking. There is no part of Amazon's algorithm that calculates the number of positive reviews into where to rank a product for search terms.

But they indirectly affect rankings because your number of reviews and star rating will impact buyer sentiment. This is why accumulating as many positive reviews as possible, especially in the beginning, is so crucial. A product with three reviews may very well lose out to a competitor who has 73 reviews. The star rating also has a great impact on sentiment. A product with four stars will likely outperform one with three.

Social proof is a major driving factor in conversion rate. Price is also a big one, but we'll get into that later. When your listings are optimized as much as possible, then you stand a greater chance of success. This is really a basic tenet for all e-commerce. The higher the percentage of people you can convince to buy your product, the greater your sales will be with fewer visitors to your web property necessary.

Two Launch Strategies

These are the most effective ways to get your product in front of people so you can start to benefit from the magic of momentum *findable* and *buyable*. Amazon sponsored product ads and blast services. I will go over both, and how best to use them for maximum results.

Amazon Sponsored Product Ads

These are also known as Amazon pay-per-click (PPC) ads. If you go to any search page on Amazon, you'll see listings that have the word "sponsored" above them, as well as listings in the right-hand sidebar. These are sponsored product ads. Sellers bid on keywords to have their listing show up in these spots. The really nifty thing about these is, when someone clicks on your ad and decides to buy, you get credit for the keyword used to find the ad. This "credit" for keywords prompts Amazon's algorithm to bump up your product's ranking.

Understanding this means you can "feed the machine" or put large amounts of money into your pay-per-click (PPC) budget to generate sales for specific keywords and increase ranking. There is an awful lot more involved, which I'll briefly touch on in a moment, but that is the general goal.

If it were as simple as putting money in to bump up your rank, everybody would be doing it, and it would come down to your marketing budget and nothing else. But, like any marketing and promotion method, you have to weigh the costs and the rewards. Sometimes people set up ad campaigns that are wildly successful. With a profitable campaign it seems like the more money you put into it, the more you make. This is true, up to a point. However, you will hit a ceiling when it comes to using up your daily budget. You will also find that your average cost per sale (the percentage indicator that tells you whether your ads are profitable) often has a sweet spot that you can slip out of if you spend too much on your ads and clicks.

And then there are campaigns that are entirely unprofitable. As in, no matter what keywords you bid on, the sales you get do not amount to enough to cover the expense. This all goes to show that using PPC is an essential strategy, but it has its limits.

When setting up PPC, make sure you do extensive keyword research and identify the most relevant and searched terms for your product. There are a number of ways to do this, but one of the best is to use Amazon's data. Run an "automatic" campaign, which is a campaign where Amazon automatically chooses keywords to bid on based on your listing. Do this for about a week and then run a keyword report. From that data, you can find good keywords by looking for keywords that generated sales. After you identify profitable keywords, set up campaigns taking advantage of *broad*, *phrase* and *exact match* keyword types.

When launching, it is entirely OK to spend "in the red" for your PPC. Basically, the higher you bid, the more likely you'll appear above your competitors on search pages. So, when launching, since your product will likely not be on page one for important search terms yet, you simply need to buy your way there. Bid higher than everyone else, and show up on the top position for ads. This may not always be profitable if you're a new seller with a new brand, but that is what I mean by spending in the red. You keep doing this until you show up on page one organically. Keep in mind, however, that PPC alone may not get you there. As I mentioned earlier, it has its limits, and your budget likely does too.

Developing a Profitable PPC Campaign

I am not going to mention PPC and then just leave it at that. While results will always vary based on category and niche competitiveness, there is a basic format that you can follow to create profitable campaigns. But first, let's identify the various keyword match options:

Broad Match—These are keywords that are matched broadly

(so it's not just a clever name). For example, if you choose the keyword "exercise bands" then broad match will likely show (based on the relevancy of your product) your sponsored product ad for keyword phrases such as "elastic exercise bands" or "20 lbs. resistance exercise bands." In broad match, the words can also appear out of order, so your ad may be shown for "bands resistance exercise." Broad match terms cast a wide net around anything and everything that's relevant and catch as many key phrases as possible.

Phrase Match—These are keywords that are matched with many other keywords, but they keep the phrase intact. So, if you use the phrase "exercise bands," your ad will get impressions for "exercise bands blue" or "strong exercise bands." The words "exercise bands" will always be in the phrase and the word order is not mixed up.

Exact Match—These are keywords that are an exact match to the words or phrase you input. So, if you are running ads for exact match keywords "exercise bands" then the ad will only show for "exercise bands." If you want your ad to be shown for "blue exercise bands" you will have to input the exact match keyword "blue exercise bands."

Negative Keywords—These are keywords that will be excluded from being shown in your campaigns. These are only relevant to broad and phrase match, but they help keep your ad from gaining needless impressions (and possible clicks) for irrelevant terms. For example, if you run broad match keywords for "potato" (maybe because you sell a potato masher) and you are getting impressions (and clicks, but no sales) for "potato gun," then you may wish to add "potato gun" to negative keywords. That way, your ad will no longer show for that term.

Now that we understand the match types, let's go over a strategy for maximizing PPC results.

As mentioned earlier, when running sponsored product ads, Amazon gives you the option to manually input keywords or run an "automatic" campaign. This is the option that allows Amazon to choose the keywords that bring up your ads. These keywords are typically based on keywords found in your listing. You'll want to run an automatic campaign for about a week to 10 days. You don't need to bid anything outrageous, but just keep a decent budget ($10 to $15 a day should be fine) so you can get enough data. This may vary by niche, however, as you do want to bid enough to at least make a few sales.

After this time period, run a keyword report (under advertising reports). This will show you every keyword customers typed into the search bar that pulled up your ad. It will also show you the ones that got the most impressions, clicks and sales. This is a fantastic resource for finding keywords that generate actual sales.

After you have identified profitable keywords (or at least keywords with high clicks, that appear to get people's attention), it's time to create some more campaigns. Turn the daily budget for your auto-campaign down to a negligible amount (you want to continue gathering data) because the rest will be manual. You'll want to create three campaigns per product. The first campaign will only have exact match keywords in it. This is where you put your profitable keywords as well as any highly searched and highly relevant keywords you uncovered through your research.

The next campaign you create will only have phrase match keywords. These need to be only two or three highly relevant phrases.

The final campaign will be for broad match keywords. These are short, but relevant one to two word keywords (like "potato" or "baby").

For the purposes of launching, you'll likely want to start by putting far more money into these campaigns than you'll sustain. That is because, as mentioned earlier, you want to buy your way to page one for as many profitable keywords as possible. In some niches you may not be able to set your budgets high enough to do this to the extreme. In others, a $200 or $300 a day budget will get you some very fast results.

When you have made the keyword movement you hoped for or feel it is time to reassess your strategy (or you run out of money), you can set your ad budgets more appropriately. You want to set your exact match budgets to the highest that makes sense. This is the campaign that uses only your profitable keywords, so your ACoS (average cost of sale) should be fairly low. I suggest putting as much money as you can afford into your daily budget for exact match, as long as your ACoS remains at a profitable level (remember ACoS only shows cost of advertising, not of your product, so you probably won't really be profitable with an ACoS higher than 40 or 50 percent). Also, bid as high as necessary to stay on page one for keywords that aren't ridiculously competitive until you rank organically on page one. Then you might want to change your bids to get on page two as well, offering multiple positions of visibility.

Your phrase and broad match campaigns, however, should have lower budgets and bids. This is because you are only setting them up to catch the occasional sale, and they are mostly there for capturing ongoing keyword data. You'll want to run a keyword report for them every month or so to identify new profitable keywords to add to your exact match campaign.

Pro Tip: Many of the successful sellers I know aren't very profitable in their PPC campaigns. The reason is because they use their ads as an opportunity for visibility. The average Amazon buyer doesn't just search, find and then purchase. Many bookmark, wishlist or otherwise wait to make the decision. Often they need to be exposed to your brand more than once before they buy. Using PPC to increase the amount of times your listing gets in front of eyeballs can still mean more sales, even if it doesn't mean lower ACoS.

Next Steps

Let's go ahead and get started developing your PPC campaign. Referring to the keyword research you did earlier, write down your choices for each type of campaign.

Broad Match:

Phrase Match:

Exact Match:

Negative Keywords:

Pricing Strategies

Obviously pricing is an important factor for any retail business. However, we will only be discussing the matter in this section as it relates to product launches. In order to fully understand how your approach to pricing can affect your launch, you must first understand the mind of the Amazon buyer.

Amazon buyers are not typically looking for the cheapest goods. They trust that Amazon is a marketplace of tremendous value, and that is what they are looking for. Usually, value will come with a great price. So in order to captivate the attention of an Amazon buyer, you must provide plenty of value.

One way to create perceived value is with premium pricing. Obviously when you are choosing a price for your product, you want to choose the highest amount you can get away with. This, however, isn't always the best way to create the momentum that will result in your company growing month over month. We must also remember that there are other factors at play on the Amazon marketplace, such as the algorithm. So what is the most effective strategy when it comes to pricing?

When launching (or relaunching) a product, a sure-fire way to gain momentum is by dropping your price to gut-wrenchingly low levels. This can be extremely hard to do, especially for the bright-eyed new seller who is totally awestruck by the 60 percent profit margin they see others getting, and they in turn expect to get. This unfortunate illusion is propagated by extremely (and accidentally) fortunate sellers.

In reality, if you reduce your price to rock-bottom levels you will create so much value that your offer becomes one people cannot refuse. How does this help you? If no one can refuse the offer, you'll get tons of sales. Keep in mind, if your margins are only 30 percent (this is as low as I like to go personally), getting a ton of sales will still net you as much money as only a few sales would at 60 percent. But there is one factor you are not considering in that scenario—conversion rate. With a super low price, your conversion rate will skyrocket. As mentioned before, conversion rate is the single most important factor in ranking to Amazon's algorithm.

You can play this pricing game as long as it takes until you are ranking "above the fold," or as close to it as possible, on page one for your major keywords. Then, every couple of days, raise your price a dollar or two. You will notice your daily sales remaining fairly consistent as you move up the price ladder. When you begin to notice a decrease in your sales and conversion, you know when to stop. The market will let you know how much your product is worth, and you'll be ranking appropriately.

Next Steps

It's time to figure out just how far you can discount your product and still feel good while increasing your conversions. Refer to the section on pricing. Jot down your start price below. Then figure out decreases in the increments listed and do a quick Amazon search for each to find out if other merchants are beating your price. You want to eventually get to the point where you are the lowest (or close to it) but still making a margin* of at least 25 percent. If you can't reach that point, that may be a sign that you need to increase your starting price.

Starting Price
Margin

30 percent reduction
Margin

35 percent reduction
Margin

40 percent reduction
Margin

45 percent reduction
Margin

50 percent reduction
Margin

55 percent reduction
Margin

60 percent reduction
Margin

65 percent reduction
Margin

70 percent reduction
Margin

75 percent reduction
Margin

80 percent reduction
Margin

*Margin equals unit price minus direct costs of producing unit (includes production, shipment, fulfillment) as a percentage of the unit price.

How to Get Product Reviews

As we discussed earlier, reviews are important to increasing conversion rates, which is important for increasing sales. Obtaining reviews can often seem like the single most important thing a seller can do. Almost every forum or grouping of Amazon private label sellers also has deeply involved conversations about how to get reviews. Basically, the perception is that it is a big deal.

I agree to a point, but I think it is taken too far. I don't think the number of reviews one has to get in order to have sufficient social proof is that great. Likely after 50 reviews a listing has proven that they are a less risky proposition. Anything beyond that is gravy, but not essential.

So how do you get those first 50 reviews? Amazon no longer allows giving away or discounting products in exchange for reviews. Because of this, review services used in the past are no longer an option for the seller who wants to stay in good standing with the marketplace.

Over time, my experience has revealed a sound strategy that can be easily implemented by the seller to obtain reviews while aligning with Amazon's terms of service:

Have an awesome follow-up sequence.

Amazon's messaging system offers sellers the ability to communicate via email with their buyers. The system exists for the purpose of following up to discuss purchase details. However, those details can include feedback.

To facilitate the automation of this process there are several third-party services that allow you to set up an "autoresponder" of sorts to communicate with your buyers. Basically, you create an automated email response sequence that will be emailed to your buyers at given intervals after their purchase.

Of course, you don't want to use this to spam your buyers (and Amazon doesn't want you to either). But you can use it as a tool to open communication, let your buyers know that you are available for support, and to solicit their feedback in the form of a product review.

Here is an example template of a two email follow-up sequences I use. The first email goes out as soon as the order is confirmed. The second goes out about a week after it is shipped.

Email 1:

Hi John,

First off, I would like to say a sincere thank you for your support. And I'd like to do it in person. So, if you'll take just a moment to view this thank you video:

< Click Here for Your Thank You Video >

Now, I just wanted to let you know that your order is being processed and you should get it soon.

When the [product] arrives, please take it for a spin. Make it work for you (don't just keep it in your closet/drawer/wherever).

Here are a few starter tips on using your new [product] right away.

Tips

The [product] should also come with instructions. If for any reason you don't receive them or have any questions, feel free to reach out.

Thanks again. You're awesome.

Email 2:

Hello again, John,

I truly hope you are thoroughly enjoying your [product]. If you did not receive it within seven days, please contact Amazon by clicking this link: http://www.amazon.com/gp/help/customer/display.html?nodeId=518316

[Personalized info about your product/brand as it relates to the buyer]

You made a great choice shopping with us. At [brand], we truly care about our customers. We are 100% dedicated to your complete satisfaction. If you have any issues, we will work with you until you're happy! That means if your customer service experience or the product is not worthy of five stars, I would really like to know about it. The only way we can grow to better serve our customers is through feedback.

And, just to make sure you are able to use your [product] to the fullest, here is an instruction video on how to get the most out of your [product name]:

< Click Here for Your Instructional Video >

As a family business, feedback is the lifeblood of our whole operation. Feedback, in the form of reviews, is the only thing that levels the playing field between small operations like [brand] and the big brands. As such, we'd like to ask you to take the time to share your experience with our company.

If you are not satisfied for ANY REASON, please contact us immediately. We want the chance to fix it and are committed to doing whatever it takes. If you have been happy with your product and customer service, we ask you to simply click the link below and type out a short description of the experience you've had. Letting other buyers know how you feel is the best way for us to spread the word and extend our offerings to the world.

Please Click Which One Pertains Most To Your Experience
A) I love it! 5 stars!
B) Good. Some Improvements Needed.
C) I Need Help.
Thank you again for being a part of this. We literally could not do it without you.

These email templates also have the company banner at the top, as well as a personalized signature and picture.

And be sure to use hyperlinks so you're not cluttering up your email with big ugly links.

Amazon does nothing to incentivize reviews. As such, reaching out to your buyers and letting them know you care and that you are available to them is a great way to get them to take the time to want to review your product.

By creating a very *human* follow-up sequence, you not only foster good will and open up the lines of communication with your buyers, but you will get reviews over time that will provide you with important feedback about your product as well as, ideally, increase your conversion rate.

Blasting Your Way to the Top

I have found that the most critical strategy for launching a product is to "blast" it. Full disclosure, I work for a service that does this. However, I'm going to lay out for you exactly how and why it works so you can come to your own conclusions.

To fully understand and appreciate what blasting a product can do, we need to dig a little deeper into how Amazon's algorithm ranks products. As I mentioned, there are a number of factors that the algorithm takes into account. First, there is relevancy, which is entirely dictated by your listing. The keywords in your title; category and browse nodes your product is cataloged under; search terms and the many fields under "more info" in your listing all help give Amazon a sense of what your product is. That creates relevancy that the algorithm will match to search terms, serving up the most relevant ones first.

But there are a lot of relevant products for every search term on Amazon, so what does the algorithm do? It ranks products by popularity. If a product gets a lot of sales as a result of a keywords search, Amazon views that as a sign that this product is what people searching for that keyword want. So, the algorithm will move that product closer to the top of the search. How this is broken down is through conversion rate. Basically someone types in a search term, then clicks on your product, then buys. If this happens repeatedly in high numbers, obviously your product is relevant and popular, so the Amazon algorithm decides it should be made easier to find. If the percentage of people finding your product and deciding to buy is also substantial, then all other things equal, your product will rise even further in rank.

Of course, the algorithm is much more complex than that. It factors in everything from search terms and listing elements, to conversion rates as a whole, conversion rates for specific search terms, sales velocity, and so much more. Understand, however, that the most significant of these factors is conversion rate followed closely by sales velocity. If your product has a stellar conversion rate, it will achieve a high rank for that search term. The missing piece to the puzzle though is making sales with as little time in between each sale as possible. That's sales velocity. If you have a great conversion rate and you make a tremendous number of sales, you'll rank even higher. Understanding this you can conclude that when you enter a search term, the number one position for that term is usually the product with the best conversion rate for that specific keyword and the most sales in the shortest amount of time (compared to other products on that page). And ZonBlast essentially offers your listing, and Amazon's algorithm, just that.

So how does a service such as ZonBlast utilize this information to help launch products? It's actually pretty simple. ZonBlast has a large list of Amazon buyers who love to purchase all sorts of goods at discounted prices. When customers "blast" a product, they provide discount codes that are distributed to this list of hungry buyers who then buy in rapid succession. They are presented the codes along with a link to the product that includes relevant keywords. The keyword embedded link essentially helps Amazon's algorithm to assign the sales velocity the product received to that keyword.

What does this produce? It produces a large number of sales with very little time in between them to a large number of people. It also assigns those sales to a specific keyword (or keywords).

Aside from the benefit of sales velocity and increased keyword power, the conversion rate increases dramatically when only the customers with the intention of buying click through to your link.

Did you catch all that? What does ZonBlast offer? Conversion boost + keyword relevance + sales velocity. That is exactly what the algorithm is looking for in order to rank products.

Given that this is such an effective means for launching, it becomes less of a matter of what you do to launch, and more of a matter of exactly how many units to use in your promotion, how to space out your promotions and what keywords to target.

In my experience, I've seen that Amazon's algorithm factors a number of sales and conversion averages over time. Hourly, daily, weekly, monthly, and six months. For this reason, I think that promoting to a large list of buyers using discount codes and spreading out the promotion for as long a period of time as possible is the best route to take. Stimulating the algorithm multiple times at regular intervals rather than only once will have a bigger impact on rank movement down the line. That is because your averages over time will constantly increase.

That said, if you have a brand-new product, the best way to wake up the algorithm is to spike it with a fairly large number of sales all at once. So for my personal strategy, I will do a single "blast" of 100 units or more for a brand-new product, followed a few days later by a sequence of multiple days in a row of promotions at a lower number of units. After four to five days of this, I'll start stretching the promotion out to every other day. All the while I'll be targeting the biggest keywords in my niche one at a time until I reach the top six in ranking for all of them.

Your promotion strategy, spacing and frequency will vary based on product and level of competition. But no matter how you achieve it, the name of the game is to get as many sales in as short a window of time as possible and to continue to do so until you are visible on several search pages and making organic sales.

The "Honeymoon Period"

In my early days as a seller I enjoyed unprecedented success in a short time after I began selling. Then suddenly, almost overnight, I ran into some challenges. I noticed that my ranking for important keywords dropped, and I could find no discernible reason why.

After scouring forums and consulting with as many fellow sellers as possible, I discovered this was common. Furthermore, I noticed a trend that newer listings seemed to overtake established listings. What could possibly be the cause? Was it that Amazon's algorithm favored newer listings by ranking them higher in the beginning?

In a way, yes.

After countless tests and digging into the data of several seller promotions, I concluded that the algorithm looks at sales velocity averages over benchmark time periods. The daily, weekly and monthly data was obvious quickly. However, this odd and sudden drop didn't make sense until it became clear that there is a benchmark for six months.

In the time before you've reached six months of selling, you are assigned a null value so your benchmarks only go as far as monthly. That means any long periods of low conversions and sales velocity won't count against you just yet.

This, basically, is your product's "honeymoon period," or period where ranking takes less effort. This is the biggest opportunity for increasing rank. So I advise that you use all the launch strategies at your disposal as soon as your product goes live. You may also consider avoiding going live until you can put your promotional strategy in place.

Launching with Your Own List

There are other launch strategies to consider. By far the most effective way to promote your business is through your own list of buyers. However, if you're just starting out you probably don't have that list yet. To a lesser degree, you may also be able to see good results from activating a community that you've grown through social media platforms.

Building a community around your brand is good for credibility and longevity. However it definitely takes time, money, effort and patience. If you have unique and engaging content, you can use paid advertising to grow your following, and then activate that following to help you with your product launch.

For example, if you sell kitchenware, you might want to build a Facebook page around the love of cooking. By running Facebook ads for page likes using Facebook's awesome targeting to only show up for people who have identified cooking as a passion, you may be able to activate those community members to help promote your brand when you want to launch your product. Hopefully, you'll also be able to get them to rush in droves to purchase your product at a discount.

A less labor-intensive way to take advantage of Facebook is to run paid advertising so it goes directly to your discount offer. Directly advertising that you have a huge discount to offer on a hot product can be an enticing thing for social surfers to click. However, this can be expensive and can take time to refine. You'll have to test multiple ad placements, images and headlines, and products are often hit or miss.

Until you've been able to successfully grow your own list of buyers, a sure-fire way to help launch your new products is to use someone else's list.

Experiments in Social Media

Facebook is often mentioned because they offer fantastic analytical information in their advertising platform. Depending on your target market, other social platforms may suit your needs better. Getting to know the driving demographics of each platform, and cross referencing that information with who your ideal customer, or "avatar," is will allow you to be where your potential customers are.

It is important to do your research and figure out where your audience is most responsive. Then find a way to add content to that medium. This may require hiring a graphic artist to create infographics for you, or you may need to dust off your old mommy blog articles. If you love taking pictures and your audience is on Instagram, you may need to get out of the house more and catalog your experiences.

When you find the social platform where your audience interacts the most, and you get comfortable interacting with them, then you can move forward with more direct strategies for building your list. Paid advertising or other marketing campaigns offer plenty of opportunity to activate a large number of followers who identify with your brand's message.

Next Steps

Take a moment to familiarize yourself with what you can do to promote yourself on Facebook (great place to start). Go ahead and put up a product page and encourage potential buyers at every opportunity to like it, so you can start building your list. Research the **Advertising** on **Facebook** and **Create Ads** sections and jot down ideas as they come to you. Put together a draft of an ad and when you feel you have a list large enough to make it worth your while, launch your Facebook campaign!

Getting Your Customers off of Amazon

One thing that Amazon wants to make abundantly clear is that your customers are *not* your customers. They are Amazon's. This is why Amazon automatically removes email addresses from messages sent through their system. They also don't allow outside links to be placed in these messages.

It's actually specifically prohibited to take any action that will lead buyers away from the Amazon website. So, if that is the case, how do you get your customers off of Amazon and onto your list?

With product inserts.

If you've ever bought something on Amazon's website from a big brand like Samsung or Panasonic, you may not have paid attention to the flyers and other promotional materials in the box. I ask you to take a second look. Do you notice something about that information? Perhaps the fact that it promotes the company's website?

While leading buyers away from Amazon is against the rules, there appears to be a grey area. Basically, whatever you put *inside* of, or include as a part of, your packaging is considered your product. And if it is your product, then it is OK to promote your brand.

That means, just like Samsung and Panasonic and countless other brands, you are allowed to include promotional material with your product. That promotional material is your number one opportunity to lead your customer to your own web property and collect their email address.

There are a few different strategies that successful sellers have employed to build their lists through inserts. I will discuss the ones I know here.

First, you must have the insert designed. You may choose to make this a simple postcard or business card. The more creative have chosen to make the insert a memorable shape. You could also make it a sticker that the buyer can then stick to something like their window or car. The more you can make your insert stand out, the more likely it is to be read.

Another tactic is to not necessarily have an insert, but if your product has a custom box, to print information on the inside cover. One colleague of mine had basically a shoebox type package, and on the underside of the lid had printed instructions on how to post a picture on Instagram with his product and receive a coupon for a future order (see Figure 6-1). Of course, the coupon is delivered by email after an email address is given.

A tactic another colleague employed was offering to enter every subscriber into a monthly draw for a $50 Amazon gift card. Obviously, the more enticing you can make the offer, the more of a response you will get.

This method will also require that you have an external web property to direct people to and a means of collecting their information. The easiest and most scalable way to handle that is with your own website and an autoresponder service like Aweber or Mailchimp, but you can leverage social platforms too.

Essentially you put forth some type of offer or reason that inspires people to give you their email address or social profile. You put that offer on or in your product packaging in the most creative way possible. Then as you sell products, you collect leads.

By enticing buyers to go to your web property and input their contact information you will effectively grow your own list of brand advocates over time that you can market to with future offers over and over again.

Figure 5-1: A promotion with instructions to post on Instagram to win free products.

Putting It All Together

Even with this amazing formula, it isn't that simple. Some niches and products are insanely competitive and a single spike to the algorithm isn't going to do much. Sometimes a brand driven niche makes it hard to get conversions up as high as they should be. And sometimes Amazon won't agree that your product is as relevant for a search term as you think it is.

So even ZonBlast has its limitations. What, then, is the most effective method of launching a product? In my experience, boosting conversion rates, relevance and sales velocity all at the same time creates the best results.

It is possible to boost sales with just one of these methods. Many people only pay for PPC ads and manage to rank for all the keywords they need to generate a large number of sales. Others merely provide the most competitive prices and manage to generate sales that way. Many people have done nothing more than blast their product at regular intervals to dominate rankings for several keywords.

But the most consistent, fastest growing, efficient and effective sellers use a combination of optimization, sponsored product ads and promotions.

Rather than eat up all of your seed money with PPC, you can use it in a bit more moderation when you combine it with other launch tactics. Rather than completely lose all of your profit margin by scraping the bottom of the pricing structure, you can find a sweet spot that gives you enough of a conversion boost while still allowing your business bank account to grow when you combine multiple launch strategies. As you can see, a combination of these methods packs the most powerful punch.

When you launch properly, you give yourself and your products the best chance for success. Every category and every product will react differently, so your specific formula of PPC to optimization to promotions will vary, but testing each one at different levels will help you optimize the equation.

A Note about Amazon's Terms of Service (TOS)

If you are already selling on Amazon, you have undoubtedly heard all manner of speculation as to the vague meaning of Amazon's constant and regular updates to their terms of service (heretofore referred to as TOS) with regards to things like "rank manipulation," "excessive giveaways," and "review manipulation."

The reason this is on so many people's minds is because it has instilled a lot of fear of crossing the line on terms when launching or promoting a product. Big companies like Amazon (and Google and Facebook, as well) have been known to not take sympathy on those who claim ignorance of their exceedingly opaque and complex terms.

That said, there have been many conversations with Amazon employees as well as interpretations from former executives that shed a bit of light on the issue. It appears Amazon has left these terms intentionally vague to allow them the latitude to go after sellers and other individuals who intentionally game and cheat their system to get ahead.

This is specifically targeting "black-hatters" or otherwise unsavory individuals who purposefully cheat by incentivizing reviews with excess inventory; have others place large quantity orders to manipulate rank; have armies of virtual assistants working for them searching for their products and placing orders that are not intended to be fulfilled for the purpose of falsely spiking Amazon's algorithm; or use fake accounts to leave reviews. These people are engaging in deceptive and harmful activities that Amazon defines as rank or review manipulation.

Promoting your product with a discount is not rank manipulation. It is promotion. This is an advertising tactic that has been used since the dawn of things being put up for sale. Using a keyword embedded URL is also not rank manipulation. Keyword embedded URLs are simply a cataloguing tool that helps Amazon know what category your product might belong in. It isn't a trick to fool their algorithm. The algorithm is complex and Amazon is smart enough to know when a listing was found organically (it's called the referring URL). Amazon "allows" keyword embedded URLs to continue to help rank listings because it helps catalog your product and it does more good than harm. If your product is not relevant to the term, it won't rank for it. If it is relevant, but the product is bad, it will not maintain conversion and therefore will rapidly fall in rank. However, if it earns a higher rank after your promotion efforts, it will stay there, generating both you and Amazon more money.

Amazon does not frown upon promotions and algorithm stimulation in this manner. Using discount promotions simply increases traffic to your listing on Amazon's website, and that increased visibility helps give your product a chance to grow sales. Amazon gives everyone the opportunity to promote their product and climb out of ranking obscurity in a number of different ways, because otherwise your product would be eternally buried under the competition. In the end, Amazon wants you to succeed, because your success means happier customers, and more money for everyone.

The most successful sellers find multiple ways to increase traffic and visibility by combining paid advertising with optimization tactics and promotions. Using inventory as a currency for marketing is just as effective as using dollars. When you find the right balance of all the necessary elements, you create a system of benefit for all involved.

This dissection of a product launch, and the components necessary for success, will give you the tools you need to get you well on your way to fully maximizing Amazon as a sales channel for your brand.

Part Six:

Amazon Terms & Communication

Listings

The terms by which Amazon sets the rules for selling on their marketplace is an understandable concern for new Amazon sellers. Anyone who has done any amount of research has probably run across a ton of horror stories—stories of a random and unexplained suspensions for no reason, or products being delisted, or any other manner of business-ending actions leaving someone who's put their entire life savings into their dream holding nothing but a bag of debt.

Most people will tell you Amazon's terms are clearly defined on their website. The truth is that even though the terms are defined, they are anything but clear. Amazon excels at providing a twisted web of vague and contradictory rules. When one section is updated another one is not, and you dare contact Seller Central to ask for clarification, you'll get a different answer five times out of five.

So what's the answer? Most people will tell you to view the rules while keeping one question in mind. *Is what I'm doing making Amazon money?* Those who give this advice believe that Amazon's top priority is making money. It's easy to think that a billion dollar corporate giant like Amazon would be aiming for this, and while their business model does leave plenty of room for them to concern themselves with profits, I'm not completely certain that pure profit is the incentive that dictates every term they put in their rules.

Amazon has a much bigger vision in mind. That vision involves becoming a large and powerful force of nature, one that isn't entirely driven by profit. When you understand what Amazon's true goal is, you can better understand how to navigate its terms.

While I do believe it's a good idea to familiarize yourself with the terms, understand that Amazon's terms are much like our laws here in the United States. Some are unnecessarily prohibitive and violations amount to those of traffic infractions. Others are taken more seriously and could lead to suspension, which is the Amazon equivalent of death row. While many a naïve Puritan will stand at their pulpit of righteousness and shame anyone who steps near a grey area of violation, you'll find that abiding by the strictest rules of Amazon is about as easy as doing the same in day-to-day life. Basically, Amazon has become so big that a lot of their terms are convoluted, redundant or unnecessary. But it is important to know which ones legitimately stand in your way and should not be violated.

When it comes to this I am far from an expert. I will do my best to not give you bad advice, but I will share my experience so you can learn from it.

First, you must understand that in the language of the terms of service Amazon makes it sound like any violation of any term is grounds for suspension. The truth is if they suspended everyone who broke the slightest rule, they wouldn't have third-party sellers.

For example, they put a lot of stern language in the verbiage about listings. While it's not a good idea to keyword the items you're listing into oblivion, following Amazon's outdated style guides might leave you in a place where your product is unattractively displayed or difficult to find in a search. If Amazon had their way, all listings would have zero sales copy in them.

So you create a listing with a title that is relevant but also does a good job of including important keywords, as well as concise bullets that do a good job of convincing your potential buyer to make the purchase. Technically you'll probably end up violating a term or two when doing this. However, it is not the end of the world. If you end up with a title or something in the bullets that Amazon doesn't like, and they find out about it, usually the worst thing they do is delist your product until you make the necessary changes. If you end up with images they don't like, usually they just switch them out for you without even saying anything. And a lot of times these changes are changes that you can fight and win back.

Multiple Seller Accounts

Another big one is setting up multiple seller accounts. Amazon comes across as pretty dramatic in its attempts to dissuade you from having more than one seller account. However, when you become a business professional you might find that you're part of several different entities, all with their own EINs, all representing different categories and different partnerships, all of which need their own selling account. Technically, every time you want to do this you're supposed to ask Amazon for permission. From my understanding they typically grant this exemption with good reason, because really, despite all of the scary language, Amazon understands that different business entities have their own unique ways of operating. That said, I've also heard they make it difficult to justify "good reason."

In my experience, if you have a different entity with a different EIN, bank account and email address, there is nothing wrong with that entity having an Amazon selling account. However, you should still adhere to Amazon's rules about having multiple accounts that sell products in the same category, effectively competing with themselves. This can be construed as gaming their system, and it won't end well if you are found out.

Pro Tip: *If you find yourself in multiple partnerships and a part of multiple entities that all have different Amazon accounts, and you are concerned about raising any red flags with Amazon, consider getting a virtual private server (VPS). VPSs offer you the ability to log into Amazon from essentially a different part of the world, so there won't be multiple accounts accessed by the same IP address.*

Alternatively, you can also have the accounts use email addresses that are separate from your main selling account with seller central permissions, thereby making you appear as a consultant for the varying companies.

Obtaining Reviews

Another big conversation topic when it comes to terms and suspension is how you go about getting reviews for your products. The terms of service explicitly state that Amazon frowns upon manipulation of the review platform. These terms are so vague you might think that giving away a coupon code to your cousin would get you suspended. In my experience, Amazon has shown the greatest amount of force in enforcing these terms when dealing with people who blatantly use "black hat" tactics. For example, Amazon does not tolerate fake orders. Amazon also does not tolerate individuals who run several buyer accounts to place real orders. Amazon does not tolerate the purchase of reviews. They also do not tolerate giving away or discounting products for reviews. They certainly do not tolerate scripts or bots that generate phantom activity for your listing. These are the activities that those terms are targeting.

Promotions

I will not say that Amazon specifically condones the use of massive promotion to rank listings. However, in my experience, this is not a violation of their terms. When you do a legitimate promotion, reducing your price significantly without making it free, money has still exchanged hands. No matter if your widget is only a dollar, Amazon still made weight handling and pick and pack fees as well as a minimum one dollar commission off of that transaction. And who decided your widget was worth more than a dollar anyway? You did. But Amazon likely does not care how much you value your product. They do care about their customers though. And I can't think of a better way to serve their customers than to give them an awesome deal.

So basically, the best way to ensure that you are in good standing with Amazon at all times is to not be greedy and do things to cheat your way to the top. Use smart promotions and marketing to drive your way to the top, yes, but do not cheat. As long as you conduct an honest and ethical business that utilizes tried-and-true marketing tactics such as giving away promotional items, asking for honest feedback, paying for advertising, and all the other ways that you can get more visibility for your product, you'll be okay. If you employ scripts, bots, fake orders, individuals with multiple buyer accounts or individuals offering the purchase of positive reviews, offer incentives for positive reviews, maliciously attack your competitors, or engage in other such blatantly unethical behavior, you run the risk of being put out of business. In the end it all boils down to common sense.

In the course of running your business you are sure to hit a question, a grey area, where even as an ethical businessperson you're going to wonder if you should take the action or not. That's when you want to look at it from Amazon's point of view. Their number one priority is the customer. It's important to them that you provide customers with a positive experience. However, if you do anything that blatantly attacks their algorithm or systems, they will not be happy. If you have a question, there are tons of groups on social media and forums with people who have experience with every facet of Amazon. Communicate with them and you're likely to find the right answer.

Talking to Amazon

But are other sellers the only people you should communicate with? There are times when the best course of action is to contact Amazon directly. Many sellers will tell you that it's better to keep a low profile and not draw attention to yourself. This is because Amazon can make mistakes, and when they make those mistakes it can be hard to correct them. The fear is if you end up on Amazon's radar and it doesn't work out for you, that could be the end. However, I personally don't like living or running my business in fear. I know the things I do are not bad, and the grey area or fine lines I walk are not business ending. The reason I'm confident in this is because my top priority is the same as Amazon's—to provide amazing value to my customers.

So for that reason I communicate with any and all departments at Amazon on a fairly regular basis. Sometimes it doesn't work out well, but I always learn something. I'm never afraid to contact Seller Central if I have a problem or question. Over time I've learned that often Seller Central is not very familiar with all of Amazon's terms. They're very bad at providing accurate definitions or otherwise outlining parameters. If you ever call or write to ask Amazon permission when it comes to a strategy, expect the answer to be "no." When you ask why, the tactic is usually that they will simply repeat your request back to you in the form of a statement saying that Amazon just doesn't allow it. Those are usually the questions you want to take to the seller communities in your network.

Otherwise any comments, concerns or questions should absolutely be brought to Amazon's attention. Learn to navigate Seller Central. Learn how to get answers through email, through chat, and on the telephone. Learn the departments. Learn that when you want to make a change to your listing you need to be forwarded directly to the feeds department. Learn that when dealing with hijackers you'll have to submit different types of infringement violations to the copyright team. Learn how frustrating it is to get the exact same cut-and-paste response ten times in a row from the copyright department. Learn how to communicate with the seller performance team or the executive seller team. It would take too long to catalog what every department does to help. The point is for you to learn. Do not be afraid to learn. Sometimes you won't be able to get anywhere with Amazon support. Sometimes being tenacious will get you exactly what you want.

Next Steps

Think back to when you created your listing. Were there any gray areas where you weren't sure what to do? Jot these down here. Then jump onto a couple of the forums listed in the Resources section in the Appendix and see what others are saying about the issue.

Conclusion

Congratulations! You've just read your way through an entire crash course in how to get started importing and selling products on Amazon. If you read straight through to the end to get an overview, then now you're ready to go back and start working through the Next Steps exercises to get your business up and running. If you've already been working through the Next Steps, then you're likely just a few clicks away from selling. Exciting isn't it?

Although you now have the nuts and bolts of how to get started in this exciting industry, there's still a lot to learn. Join a few forums, do your own research and stay tuned for our next book that will drill down into some of the finer points of selling. This is a fascinating world you've entered into. It's always in motion. There are always new opportunities. By carefully applying well-researched material such as this book and using your own business acumen (common sense), you will find yourself on the road to your dream quicker than you ever could have imagined.

Best of luck!

Appendix

Useful Information

Duties and Tariffs

Duty/Tariff—Tax paid on commodity goods imported or otherwise brought into another country. A "toll."

HS/HTS Code—This stands for Harmonized System or Harmonized Tariff System, which is the system of codes by which commodity duty rates are classified per country. This typically 10-digit code will classify the goods you are bringing into the country and assign your duty rate accordingly.

You can find your product's HS code by running a search for your commodity on these sites:

hts.usitc.gov/

foreign-trade.com/reference/hscode.htm

dutycalculator.com/

Safety Certifications

As an importer, it is your responsibility to determine whether your product requires safety or other certifications before being sold in your country. Here are a few you may run into for the U.S.:

CPSIA—Consumer Product Safety Improvement Act, generally regulates all children's products. The Consumer Product Safety

Commission website (cpsc.gov) states the following:

The CPSIA defines the term "children's product" and generally requires that children's products:

1. Comply with all applicable children's product safety rules;

2. Be tested for compliance by a CPSC-accepted accredited laboratory, unless subject to an exception;

3. Have a written Children's Product Certificate that provides evidence of the product's compliance; and

4. Have permanent tracking information affixed to the product and its packaging where practicable.

There are also a number of non-children products that must issue a GCC (General Certificate of Conformity). This information is found on the Consumer Product Safety Commission website (cpsc.gov).

FDA—The Food and Drug Administration requires compliance with a number of rule sets for all consumables and cosmetics that are imported. So long as your goods comply with FDA regulation (fda.gov/) and consumables/cosmetics are manufactured in facilities that are registered with the FDA, no additional certification is required. Just make sure that your supplier is registered and familiar with U.S. laws and your forwarder is aware that they will need to contact the FDA before the arrival of your goods.

Trademark Considerations

Trademarking is a necessary and important step for the future growth of your business, but may not be mission critical at the outset. There are many ways to complete trademarking, just keep in mind what it is that you will be registering. Every word or symbol or stylized phrasing will need its own trademark. While you can certainly file the necessary paperwork on your own, you may consider hiring a professional (such as Trademarkia) to handle it for you. They will be able to help you to know what things you should register as well as help discover whether your potential trademark already exists.

Resources

B2B Sites

alibaba.com

globalsources.com

hktdc.com

made-in-china.com

ttnet.com

Build Your Own Website

shopify.com

squarespace.com

wordpress.com

Design Services and Other Freelance Labor

99designs.com

fiverr.com

peopleperhour.com

upwork.com

Forums

sellercentral.amazon.com/forums/index.jspa

facebook.com/groups/SmartChinaSourcing/

facebook.com/groups/842740675773044/

facebook.com/groups/AmazonPPC/

facebook.com/groups/AmazonVeterans/

facebook.com/groups/amzclassroom/?ref=group_browse_new

facebook.com/groups/ecomazon/?ref=group_browse_new

How to Find a Top Selling Product

bestsellingauctions.com

watchcount.com

Inspection Service

asiainspection.com

richforth.com/home.html

Keyword Research

adwords.google.com/keywordplanner

google.com/trends

keywordinspector.com

merchantwords.com

Logistics Company

bgiworldwide.com

chrobinson.com/en/us/

Miscellaneous

JungleScout (junglescout.com/)—Most accurate sales estimator out there, with a bunch of other cool features that will help you as a seller.

Private Label Podcast (privatelabelpodcast.com/)—If you are looking for a fantastic resource for great information on the evolution of the private label business, this podcast is it.

Products on White Photography (powproductphotography.com/)—A personal favorite for stunning product shots on a white background.

WYSIWYG Editor (bestonlinehtmleditor.com)—Html editor.

ZonBlast (zonblast.com/)—Far and away the most effective launch service that allows you to use your inventory as currency for advertising. ZonBlast guarantees increased search ranking for relevant keywords you choose.

Zonsquad (zonsquad.com/)—Mastermind group for Amazon private label sellers. This paid community gives you access to some of the greatest minds in the industry.

Setting up a Business

legalzoom.com

mycorporation.com/business-formations/llc.jsp

irs.gov (for EIN)

Vendor Letter Templates

Template No.1

Dear [Supplier]

My name is [Name] and I represent [Company]. We are a successful e-commerce enterprise selling over [Sales Figure] a year on Amazon.com. Our products are primarily in the [Niche] and we think that your [Product] would be a good addition to our catalog. We have been very successful in creating a demand for our brand and are confident your product will be a success.

I just have a couple of questions for you:

1. What is your production time?

2. Can we stitch/imprint our logo on the product itself?

3. Are you the manufacturer?

4. Do you offer custom packaging (color box)?

5. Do you have a sample we can order?

Right now we are taking samples from a few factories and will make the decision to work with a factory based on the quality. I am impressed with your presentation so far and hope to hear from you further.

Sincerely,

This will only work if you already have a brand and decent sales figures. Even if you only sell a few thousand dollars a month, you can say "we sell over a quarter of a million dollars a year." However, if you are just starting out, you may wish to use this approach:

Template No.2

Dear [Supplier]

My name is [Name] and I represent [Company], a startup brand gaining traction in the [Niche] here in the U.S. We are looking to expand our presence online and wish to flesh out our brand with quality [Niche] products like your [Product].

The rest remains the same.

And if you are looking to move into a completely different niche you can use this:

Template No.3

Dear [Supplier]

My name is [Name] and I represent [Company], a successful American [Niche] brand. We are looking to expand into the [New Niche] space and see your [Product] as a fantastic opportunity to do so.

The rest remains the same.

The purpose of these five questions is to get to the heart of what is important. If you get to the heart of what is important, then the supplier will probably take you seriously. Everybody inquires about price. Large importers, however, are much more concerned with quality, as they have an idea already of what to expect with price.

Production time, while likely always longer than you want, is important to know so you can successfully set up your logistics. You also need to know if you can brand the product, because if you can't, you probably want to move on. While dealing directly with the manufacturer isn't necessary, it is a plus. This makes it easier for you to make structural changes should the need ever arise. Custom packaging is also important. One of the simplest ways to set yourself apart and make your brand seem more "premium" is with custom packaging. The final question is how you get the ball rolling. Asking for a sample means you are interested in assessing the quality. Go through the process to get all the way to a sample and then order a few. Based on the quality you will then know who you wish to proceed to the next step with.

After getting a few samples, you'll want to follow up with your suppliers:

Template No.4

Dear [Supplier]

I just wanted to inform you that we have received your sample and tested its quality. I'd also like to inform you that we are impressed and it will be a consideration in our final decision. We are currently testing just a few of your competitor's samples, but your [Product] is a superior one.

I would now like to ask, when it is convenient, can you provide me with a quote for 5,000 units of [Product] FOB including the custom logo and package modifications we discussed?

I will take the quote to my partners and we will make our final decision promptly.

After you receive a quote for a few thousand units, you'll want to haggle the price down. The best way to do this is by pitting a competitor against them (even if you don't have a competing offer).

Template No.5

Dear [Supplier]

Thank you for the quote and prompt reply. I have presented it to my partners and we are still testing samples but are close to a final decision.

I will tell you, I personally prefer your [Product]. I think it is of superior quality and I also prefer your communication style (you are very prompt). However, one of your competitors has offered us a more attractive price.

Their quality is comparable and their pricing is a bit lower. My partners are almost ready to move forward with them, but I have asked to wait a bit longer to make some other considerations.

I would really like to work with you, but I wonder if you can match their price of $X per unit. I know it is lower, but if you can match it, then I can almost guarantee we'll be placing a bulk order with you.

I look forward to your reply and I appreciate your diligence. I hope we will be able to work together further.

Glossary

Glossary

B2B—business to business. A company that connects suppliers with buyers.

BSR—best seller rank.

Bridge site—a website that creates a bridge between the supplier and buyer. Also referred to as B2B.

Customs—the department you deal with when importing goods from overseas.

DDP—delivered duty paid.

Duty—the fee you pay to import goods from overseas.

EIN—employer ID number.

FBA—Fulfillment by Amazon.

FCL—full container load.

HS code—harmonized system code, also HTS or harmonized tariff system code, is the system of codes by which commodity duty rates are classified per country. This 10-digit code will classify the goods you are bringing into the country and assign your duty rate accordingly.

FOB—the most common way you'll have your goods imported. Stands for "free-on-board" which simply means your supplier is responsible for getting your goods onto the craft that brings your goods overseas.

Freight Forwarder—the logistics company that will help you import your goods.

Infographic—a graphic visual representation of information, data or knowledge intended to present information quickly and clearly.

LCL—less than a container load.

PPC—pay-per-click. This typically refers to Amazon Sponsored Product Ads.

ODM—original design manufacturer.

OEM—original equipment manufacturer.

Pick and pack fee—fee charged by Amazon when you sell an item.

SKUs—stock keeping units. A store's or catalog's product and service identification code, often portrayed as a machine-readable bar code that helps the item to be tracked for inventory.

Tariff code—see HS code.

Third-party sellers—sellers who sell the product themselves through a fulfillment channel such as Amazon.

Weight handling fee—fee charged by Amazon when you sell an item.

White label—produced by one company that other companies rebrand to make it appear as if they had made it.

WYSIWYG—what you see is what you get.

Index

Index

Acknowledgements

This book, or my portion of it, is dedicated to the Clan, my personal tribe and mastermind, without whom I'd have no idea what on earth I was doing. The five other members of this amazing group have helped me through every challenge that has come to greet me.

I'd also like to acknowledge all the amazing people I've met in this industry. My friends from the Ukraine, Romania, Hong Kong, the UK, Germany, the Netherlands and even Minnesota. Their perspectives have enlightened me so much. I always have something new to test and my business has definitely grown as a result.

Special thanks to Ryan Moran because without that Facebook video I would have never discovered this wonderful opportunity and met the people I've had the pleasure of meeting.

And of course, Andrea, Dyana and Atlantis, the loves of my life. You provide me with my reason. My why. That is what keeps these projects moving forward.

And extra special thanks to my amazing editor and partner Dana. This book and all future books would literally not exist if not for.

Anthony Lee

I'd like to acknowledge the unfailing support and design expertise of David Barfield who was always willing to drop everything to make sure this book came into being.

A huge thanks to my parents who have always believed in me and my dreams no matter how obscure they may seem, my brother Brian Smith for his support, technical and otherwise, and to my dear friend and mentor Jeffrey Koterba who is always there no matter what.

And a heartfelt thanks to the amazing personality behind this project, Anthony, who saw a future in a random meeting on an hour-long flight and followed up.

Dana Barfield

Made in the USA
Middletown, DE
18 February 2018